The Community of the Book

A Directory of Selected Organizations and Programs

Second Edition

Compiled by Maurvene D. Williams

Edited and with an Introduction by
John Y. Cole
Director, The Center for the Book

Library of Congress
Washington
1989

Library of Congress Cataloging-in-Publication Data

Williams, Maurvene D.
 The community of the book : a directory of organizations and
programs / compiled by Maurvene D. Williams ; edited and with an
introduction by John Y. Cole (The Center for the Book). — 2nd ed.
 p. cm.

 Rev. ed. of: The community of the book / compiled by Carren O.
Kaston. 1986.
 Includes bibliographical references and index.
 ISBN 0-8444-0635-X
 ____ _____ Copy 3. Z663 .118.C65 1989
 1. Bibliography—United States—Societies, etc.—Directories.
2. Book industries and trade—United States—Societies, etc.—
Directories. 3. Books and reading—United States—Societies, etc.—
Directories. 4. Library science—United States—Societies, etc.—
Directories. 5 Literacy—United States—Societies, etc.—
Directories. I. Cole, John Young, 1940– . II. Kaston, Carren,
1946– The community of the book. III. Center for the Book.
IV. Title.
Z1008.K38 1989
002'.06073—dc19

Contents

Preface

On December 5, 1988, President Ronald Reagan officially proclaimed 1989 as "The Year of the Young Reader" in the United States. In January 1989 Mrs. Barbara Bush, the wife of President George Bush agreed to serve as honorary chairperson for the Year of the Young Reader. Initiated by the Library of Congress through its Center for the Book and its Children's Literature Center, "1989—The Year of the Young Reader" is a national campaign to encourage the love of books and reading among young people. Many of the organizations listed in this directory are participating in this effort, which emphasizes the importance of introducing books and reading to children at an early age.

The Community of the Book: A Directory of Selected Organizations and Programs, describes organizations that promote books and reading, administer literacy projects, and encourage the study of books. It focuses on national programs of special interest to the Center for the Book but was compiled to be useful to the entire book community. The emphasis is on the United States, where recently there has been renewed interest in educational reform, in literacy, in reading, and in "the future of the book." Many international book organizations and programs are included, but such coverage is limited. We hope future editions of this directory can be broader in scope, both nationally and internationally.

The Center for the Book in the Library of Congress was established in 1977 to stimulate public interest in books, reading, and the printed word. The projects and publications of the center and its seventeen state affiliates are supported by tax-deductible contributions from individuals, corporations, and foundations. Special thanks for this publication go to compiler Maurvene D. Williams and to Anne Boni, who helped prepare the manuscript for publication.

John Y. Cole
Director
The Center for the Book
February 1989

1989 YEAR OF THE YOUNG READER
LIBRARY OF CONGRESS

Is There a Community of the Book?

An Introduction
John Y. Cole

Is there a "community of the book?" The Center for the Book in the Library of Congress was established in 1977 on the assumption that such a community exists and that it can be mobilized to keep books and reading central to our personal lives and to the life of our democracy. A national partnership between the Library of Congress and private citizens and organizations, the Center for the Book stimulates public awareness and appreciation of books, reading, and libraries.

The most important person in this partnership or community is the individual reader. Former Librarian of Congress Daniel J. Boorstin, the center's founder, made this clear when the center was created, saying, "As the national library of a great free republic, the Library of Congress has a special duty and a special interest to see that books do not go unread...here we shape plans for a grand national effort to make all our people eager, avid, understanding, critical readers."[1] In "A Nation of Readers," a talk he presented in 1982, Boorstin asserted that our country was built on books and reading and that, at least in the past, America has been a nation of readers.[2] We can be so again, he maintains, if our citizens and institutions make a new commitment to keeping "the culture of the book" thriving.[3] In this effort, which is the basic mission of the Center for the Book, technology is an ally: "We have a special duty to see that the book is the useful, illuminating servant of all other technologies, and that all other technologies become the effective, illuminating acolytes of the book."[4]

Publisher Samuel S. Vaughan, in his essay "The Community of the Book" in the Winter 1983 issue of *Daedalus*, defines the book community as one that "consists of those for whom the written word, especially as expressed in printed and bound volumes, is of the first importance." Its major inhabitants are authors, editors, publishers, booksellers, librarians, wholesalers, literary agents and literary critics, book reviewers and book journalists, translators, educators, and "not least, though often omitted from full partnership—readers." Vaughan challenges many common assertions about books and publishing, including his own basic assumption:

> It is convenient to think of ourselves as the Community of the Book. But perhaps we are destined to remain a series of separate states, warring factions, shouting imprecations at each other across borders...I hope not. For we are bound up in common concerns and causes; we do need each other, and for the usual reasons—because we are mutually dependent.[5]

5

The search for a "book community" in the United States is not new. The story in recent decades is a mixture of solid accomplishments and periods of frustration, a reflection of both the tenuous nature of alliances among book-minded people and traditional American uncertainty about the proper role of government in culture, education, and the world of books.[6]

In 1950 a small group of leading American publishers, including Cass Canfield of Harper & Row, Curtis McGraw from McGraw-Hill, Harold Guinzburg of Viking Press, and Douglas Black of Doubleday and Company, established the American Book Publishers Council (ABPC), a trade association that would extend itself beyond usual business concerns in order to promote books, reading, and libraries. The first discussions between ABPC representatives and librarians took place at the 1950 annual conference of the American Library Association (ALA). Postal rates, book distribution, copyright, and reading promotion were early agenda items.[7] The anthology *The Wonderful World of Books* (1952) was a result of the 1951 Conference on Rural Reading, sponsored by the ABPC, the U.S. Department of Agriculture, the ALA, and other organizations. Theodore Waller, the first managing director (1950-53) of the ABPC, and Dan Lacy, who succeeded Waller and guided the ABPC's affairs until he joined McGraw-Hill in 1966, were the key figures in forging these early book world alliances.

Censorship became a topic of mutual concern to publishers and librarians in the early 1950s, when private groups and public officials in various parts of the country made attempts to remove books from sale, to censor textbooks, to distribute lists of "objectionable" books or authors, and to purge libraries. Senator Joseph R. McCarthy's Senate Subcommittee on Investigations, for example, demanded that the overseas information libraries of the State Department be purged of books that presented "pro-Communist" views. In response, in May 1953 the ALA and the ABPC sponsored a conference on the Freedom to Read. Librarian of Congress Luther H. Evans chaired the two-day meeting, which resulted in substantial agreement on principles and soon led to a Freedom to Read Declaration that was adopted by both associations. The American Booksellers Association, the Book Manufacturers' Institute, the National Council of Teachers of English, and other groups soon added their endorsements.

The Freedom to Read Declaration and related intellectual freedom issues united publishing and library leaders and their organizations and stimulated, in 1954, the creation of the National Book Committee. Declaring itself a citizen-oriented, public interest voice on behalf of books, the book committee urged the "wider distribution and wider use" of books and encouraged greater use and support of libraries, the development of lifelong reading habits, improved access to books, and the freedom to read. Its approximately three hundred members worked together and with the professional book community to "foster a general public understanding of the value of books to the individual and to a democratic society."

The American Book Publishers Council and the American Library Association, the primary sponsors of the National Book Committee, provided the committee with its small, paid professional staff and with office space. Most of its projects were supported by grants from foundations or by government funds. In 1955 a Commission on the Freedom to Read was established. In 1958 the book committee inaugurated National Library Week, a year-round promotion and media campaign that encouraged citizen support for libraries, which it administered in collaboration with the ALA for the next sixteen years. In 1960 the committee began administering the National Book Awards, which honored American books of literary merit and their authors. For the next decade the committee initiated and cosponsored, with a wide variety of organizations, useful conferences on topics such as the development of lifelong reading habits, the role of U.S. books abroad, books in the schools, the need for books in rural areas as well as in urban slums, the need to strengthen school libraries, and the public library in the city. The book committee also guided development of a "Reading Out Loud" educational television series, which was produced by the Westinghouse Broadcasting Company, and sponsored the initial publication of enduring classics such as Nancy Larrick's *Parent's Guide to Children's Reading* and G. Robert Carlsen's *Books and the Teen-Age Reader.*[8]

The National Book Committee's sponsorship of projects and publications about the role of American books overseas, particularly in Asia and Africa, reflected widespread recognition of the key role that books could play in economic and cultural development. American government officials, publishers, educators, and librarians established several important programs that stimulated book exports, foreign trade, and international exchange; encouraged publishing in developing countries; and promoted books, libraries, and reading around the world. The major efforts were the Informational Media Guaranty Program (IMG) (1948-68), a program which borrowed funds from the U.S. Treasury to enable United States book publishers, as well as producers of other "informational media" such as films and recordings, to sell their materials in countries that were short of hard-currency foreign exchange; Franklin Book Programs, Inc. (1952-79), a nonprofit, private educational corporation initiated by the publishing community and supported by U.S. government information agencies and foundations to "assist developing countries in the creation, production, distribution, and use of books and other educational materials"; and the Government Advisory Committee on Book and Library Programs (1962-77), a panel of publishers, booksellers, and librarians that met with government officials to provide advice about federal book policies and programs.[9]

Unesco proclaimed the year 1972 as International Book Year in order to "focus the attention of the general public (and of) governments and international and domestic organizations on the role of books and related materials in the lives and affairs of the individual and society." The National Book Committee organized and supported U.S. participation in International Book Year. The year 1972 was a high watermark in the United States for cooperative organizational efforts on behalf of books and reading. Two years later the National Book Committee itself was disbanded; in 1977 the Government Advisory Committee on Book and Library Programs was abolished; and in 1979 Franklin Book Programs was formally liquidated. Thus in 1982, when

Unesco sponsored a World Congress on Books to assess international progress in promoting books since 1972, several of the key United States organizations that had participated in International Book Year were gone.

What had happened to the programs that made the 1960s and early 1970s such a productive period of cooperation in the United States book community? The Informational Media Guaranty Program was terminated in 1968 when the U.S. Congress, concerned about the large indebtedness to the U.S. Treasury incurred by the IMG program, denied funds to the United States Information Agency for the program's administration. According to publisher Curtis G. Benjamin, the final controversy over the method of funding IMG was only one of a long series of misunderstandings: "to some [IMG] was a government propaganda device, to others it was a subsidy of commercial exporters, and to still others it spelled censorship." Benjamin, writing in 1984, expressed his hope "that a new (and much simplified) IMG-type program will somehow and soon be organized to meet the challenges that are today as critical as they were in the last decades following World War II."[10]

The National Book Committee was formally dissolved on November 15, 1974. Several related problems had become insurmountable. These included inflationary increases in costs, drastically lessened support from the publishing industry, and the committee's inability to raise basic operating funds from sources outside publishing. In December 1972, the committee had lost the funding and support through services in kind it previously had received from the Association of American Publishers (the successor to the American Book Publishers Council). This separation, according to John C. Frantz, the book committee's former executive director, "came at the worst time in the Book Committee's financial affairs." Other problems also plagued the committee, including management difficulties and disagreements among publishers and librarians about the administration of major projects such as the National Book Awards. A fundamental fund-raising difficulty, according to Frantz, was the committee's inability "to overcome its apparently incompatible, not to say schizoid, origins" and reach far enough beyond the library and publishing professions "to achieve a separate, clearly defined identity."[11] In a parting tribute that called attention to "many fine things" that had happened to books and reading because of the National Book Committee, the editors of *Publishers Weekly* ruefully noted that "some day it will have to be reinvented."[12]

The Government Advisory Committee on Book and Library Programs not only had advisory and review functions but also was a valuable forum for discussing programs of mutual concern to the government and the private sector, for example, international copyright, tariffs on educational books, and overseas distribution of American scientific books. It also supported Unesco initiatives such as the International Book Year. In 1977, however, President Jimmy Carter asked that all "nonessential" government advisory groups be abolished. The State Department, citing the reduced role that books and libraries by then were playing in the programs of the United States Information Agency and the U.S. Agency for International Development and noting an increased private sector role in international book activity, recommended that the advisory committee be terminated. This recommendation was accepted in April 1977, and the committee was abolished.

By 1977 Franklin Book Programs, Inc., a significant venture in international publishing that used government and private funds, was also struggling for existence. The major reason was rapidly decreasing support from the United States Information Agency, which had helped fund Franklin from its beginning, but Franklin also faced internal financial and management difficulties, particularly in certain overseas field offices. The United States Information Agency had also become increasingly particular about which publications it would subsidize, causing controversy and ill will between Franklin representatives and government officials. According to Curtis G. Benjamin, Franklin Books forfeited much of its U.S. government support by "refusing to limit its sponsorship to books that were strictly in line with U.S. foreign policy objectives as interpreted by U.S. Information Agency program officers."[13] Franklin had financed its operating costs by its own earnings and by contributions from United States foundations, corporations, and individuals through overhead allowances from grants and contracts. With government and foundation interest in its activities sharply decreased, in October 1977 Franklin Book's board of directors suspended all operations.

The decision to close the corporation came the next year and liquidation was completed in 1979. Franklin's remaining cash balance and receivables, amounting to less than ten thousand dollars, were contributed to the Center for the Book in the Library of Congress.

Change in leadership in publishing and librarianship in the 1960s was one reason why cooperative attitudes began to fade. For example, Dan Lacy, a consistent champion of closer cooperation between publishers and librarians, left the American Book Publishers Council in 1966. Industry leaders after Lacy did not feel as strongly about the importance of publisher-librarian cooperation. Economic pressures in the late 1960s and early 1970s also had an effect. Publishers raised prices to meet increased costs, and as the rate of inflation increased, librarians looked to resource sharing, networking, and more selective book-buying to stretch their limited acquisitions budgets.

Copyright, however, was the single most important issue in the deterioration of publisher-librarian relations, and it rapidly became the central divisive issue. A bill for a proposed revision of the copyright law, introduced in 1965, grew more controversial as a decade of hearings progressed, with a few publishers actually going so far as to conclude that "the photocopy machine in the hands of a librarian is the most serious threat to the survival of the publishing industry."[14] The new Copyright Law of 1976 did not stop disputes about "fair use" or decrease uncertainty about the effects of new technological changes.

According to economist Robert W. Frase, "Wall Street discovered book publishing" in the mid-1960s, mainly because of the "well-publicized increases in federal support for education and libraries" during the administration of

President Lyndon B. Johnson.[15] Conglomerates such as CBS, MCA, Gulf & Western, the Times-Mirror Corporation, and Xerox gradually entered the industry. The book-publishing business expanded in the 1970s, but the absorption, or in some cases the attempted absorption, of smaller firms by large conglomerates brought forth charges of "undue concentration" from the Authors Guild, which felt that such mergers threatened the "very existence" of the book community. The dispute was aired at congressional hearings held on March 13, 1980, where Senator Howard M. Metzenbaum went a step further and expressed his concern about "greater and greater concentration" in the bookselling business as well.[16]

The growth of publishing and communication conglomerates heightened distrust. The increased size of many publishing firms was seen by sociologist Lewis Coser, for example, as one reason why so many publishers and major editors seemed to be "losing contact with the world of creative intellect." Coser felt that to the extent that publishers and editors were separated from authors by agents and others, they were likely "to let their general cultural responsibilities remain on the back burner, while the front burner is occupied by business considerations and calculations."[17]

If in the 1970s publishing as a profession turned inward toward business considerations, the library profession continued its inward drive toward further specialization and thus fragmentation. The technological revolution, symbolized by the establishment in 1971 of the first computer-based, online cataloging system, captured the attention of librarians and became a dominant force in the profession. Neither publishers nor librarians seemed able to reach very far beyond their own immediate problems or concerns. Since by then government was in a period of retrenchment, at least in terms of support for education and cultural activities, the decade was an inauspicious time for undertaking cooperative endeavors that would enhance the role of the book in the general culture. Several publishers recognized the need, however. Writing in the April 1977 issue of *Scholarly Publishing*, Herbert S. Bailey, director of the Princeton University Press, explained that while the book community

> should be working together for the advancement of scholarship and for the good of society, we seem to be separated by a system that puts authors and publishers and booksellers and librarians and finally readers in opposition to each other, so that we often offend each other in seeking our individual interests—in copyright, in selecting publications, in making academic appointments, in purchasing, in the prices we charge, [and] in the uses we make of books.[18]

A modest step was taken in the fall of 1977. At the urging of Librarian of Congress Daniel J. Boorstin, Congress created the Center for the Book in the Library of Congress. Boorstin, a historian who became Librarian of Congress in 1975, was eager for the institution to play a more prominent role in the national culture. In an article in *Harper's* written before he became Librarian of Congress, he had explained in detail why "the book" was the best "do-it-yourself, energy-free communication device" ever invented.[19] The development of a new national office at the Library of Congress for promoting books was a natural action for Boorstin. Representative Lucien N. Nedzi of Michigan and Senator Howard Cannon of Nevada, the chairman and cochairman of the Joint Committee on the Library, cosponsored the necessary legislation. The center was established by Public Law 95-129, approved on October 13, 1977, in which the U.S. Congress affirmed its belief in "the importance of the printed word and the book" and recognized the need for continued study of the book and the written record as "central to our understanding of ourselves and our world." President Jimmy Carter approved the legislation to indicate his "commitment to scholarly research and the development of public interest in books and reading."[20]

The new law authorized the Center for the Book to use private, tax-deductible contributions to support its program and publications. Thus the new organization was founded as a true partnership between government and the private sector. Its initial planning meetings and programs were supported by two generous private donors: McGraw-Hill, Inc., and Mrs. Charles W. Engelhard. Over a dozen people who had been closely associated with the National Book Committee, the Government Advisory Committee on International Book and Library Programs, and Franklin Book Programs became valuable members of the Center for the Book's first National Advisory Board, and their previous experiences helped shape the center's early programs.

There are important differences, however, between the Center for the Book and its organizational predecessors, and perhaps these differences will help ensure a long life for the center. The creation of the Center for the Book was supported by the U.S. Congress and endorsed by the President. The center has the authority of a government agency and enjoys the prestige of being part of the Library of Congress, a unique and most appropriate home for such an endeavor. But it does not depend on government funding for its program; in fact more than half its total annual budget comes from private contributions from individuals and corporations. Thus the center has a practical, project-oriented character that is tailored to specific activities which outside donors are willing to support. Finally, the center serves as a catalyst—a source of ideas—and a forum but not as an administrator of major programs or long-term projects. Its full-time staff has never exceeded three people. Thus, while it is part of a large and prestigious government institution that also happens to be the world's largest library, the Center for the Book itself is small and flexible, two desirable traits in the fragile and always changing community of the book.

A Nation at Risk, the 1983 report prepared by the National Commission on Excellence in Education, helped revive national interest in education and learning. A "call to arms" that provoked educators and citizens alike, the report stimulated both an education reform movement and increased private sector involvement in literacy projects and education programs. The Center for the Book's major contributions during this period of renewed interest in books and reading have been the publication of the results of its The Book in the Future project—*Books in Our Future: A Report from the Librarian of*

Congress (1984) and *Books in Our Future: Perspectives and Proposals* (1987)—and the publication of this directory, which first appeared in 1986.

The catalytic function of the Center for the Book has expanded dramatically since 1984 with the establishment of statewide, affiliated centers for the book in seventeen states or regions of the United States. The purpose of each state center is to stimulate interest in books and reading and in all parts of a state's "book culture," from author through reader. Each state center develops and funds its own operations and projects. Each also uses national promotion themes developed by the Library of Congress center, themes such as "1987—The Year of the Reader," "1989—The Year of the Young Reader," "Read More About It," "Books Make a Difference," "A Nation of Readers," and "To Read Out Loud!" When its application is approved, a state center for the book is granted affiliate status for a period of three years. The seventeen state centers and their dates of establishment are Arizona (1988), California (1987), Colorado (1988), Connecticut (1987), Florida (1984, renewed 1987), Illinois (1985, renewed 1988), Indiana (1987), Iowa (1987), Kansas (1987), Michigan (1986), Ohio (1987), Oklahoma (1986), Oregon (1986), Upper Midwest (Minnesota, North Dakota, South Dakota, 1986), Texas (1987), Virginia (1987), and Wisconsin (1986).

At the beginning of 1989 it is clear that there are signs of revival in the book community. Small presses are proliferating and the book business itself is thriving. There is renewed private sector interest in literacy and education. In addition to an expanding national Center for the Book network, the U.S Information Agency has reinstated its Book and Library Advisory Committee and the National Book Awards, Inc., which became a nonprofit organization in 1987, has expanded its interests to include reading promotion and "wider public participation in the literary arts." Many uncertainties remain, however. Mergers in publishing have continued, often exacerbating the inherent conflicts in the book industry between commerce and culture, between profit and quality. Book distribution is still a major problem. And serious interest in research still lags. The Center for Book Research at the University of Scranton, a promising research center established in 1983, closed in 1988 because of lack of adequate financial support.

This directory, nonetheless, describes the activities of 100 organizations, 11 more than were included in the first edition (1986). Taken together, the efforts of these one hundred organizations are at the core of the "community of the book" in the United States, at least as seen from the Center for the Book in the Library of Congress at the beginning of 1989. May our number continue to expand!

Notes

1. John Y. Cole, *The Center for the Book in the Library of Congress: The Planning Year* (Washington: Library of Congress, 1978), 5-6.

2. Daniel J. Boorstin, *A Nation of Readers* (Washington: Library of Congress, 1982).

3. Joint Committee on the Library, Congress of the United States, *Books in Our Future: A Report from the Librarian of Congress to the Congress* (Washington: Library of Congress, 1984), letter of transmittal.

4. Cole, *The Center for the Book in the Library of Congress: The Planning Year*, 5-6.

5. Samuel S. Vaughan, "The Community of the Book," *Daedalus* 112 (Winter 1983): 112. For another perspective on "the shared responsibilities of the book community," see Ann Heidbreder Eastman, "Books, Publishing, Libraries in the Information Age," *Library Trends* 33 (Fall 1984): 121-47.

6. In learning about events in the United States book community from the 1950s to the present, the author has profited from discussions with many of the key participants, including Dan Lacy, Theodore Waller, Robert W. Frase, Virginia Mathews, Ann Heidbreder Eastman, and Carol A. Nemeyer.

7. Theodore Waller, "The United States Experience in Promoting Books, Reading, and the International Flow of Information," in John Y. Cole, ed., *The International Flow of Information: A Trans-Pacific Perspective* (Washington: Library of Congress, 1981), 14.

8. Waller, "The United States Experience," 15-16.

9. Curtis G. Benjamin, *U.S. Books Abroad: Neglected Ambassadors* (Washington: Library of Congress, 1984), 17, 24-25, 34-38.

10. Benjamin, *U.S. Books Abroad*, 20-21.

11. John C. Frantz, "A Death in the Family," *American Libraries* 6 (April 1975): 206.

12. Editorial, "We Shall Miss the National Book Committee," *Publishers Weekly*, December 2, 1974, 15.

13. Benjamin, *U.S. Books Abroad*, 26.

14. Jay K. Lucker, "Publishers and Librarians: Reflections of a Research Library Administrator," *Library Quarterly* 54 (January 1984): 50.

15. Robert W. Frase, tape cassette statement to John Y. Cole, October 2, 1985.

16. John Y. Cole, ed., *Responsibilities of the American Book Community* (Washington: Library of Congress, 1981), 24.

17. Lewis A. Coser, "The Private and Public Responsibilities of the American Publisher," in ibid., 15.

18. Herbert S. Bailey, Jr., "Economics of Publishing in the Humanities," *Scholarly Publishing* 8 (April 1977): 223-24.

19. Daniel J. Boorstin, "A Design for an Anytime, Do-It-Yourself, Energy Free Communication Device," *Harper's*, January 1974, 83-86.

20. 91 Stat. 1151; *Library of Congress Information Bulletin* 36 (October 21, 1977), 717. Boorstin's initiative was reinforced by a 1976 report of a publishers' advisory group, chaired by Dan Lacy of McGraw-Hill, which called on the Library of Congress to strengthen its activities "in relation to the role of the book in American culture." See John Y. Cole, ed., *The Library of Congress in Perspective* (New York: Bowker, 1978), 240-42.

How to Use This Directory

Maurvene D. Williams

The Community of the Book is intended to serve as a guide to many of the major organizations and programs whose purposes and interests overlap with those of the Center for the Book. Publishers, booksellers, librarians, book researchers, scholars, teachers, and writers are among those represented here by a selective listing of their professional organizations and associations. Directory entries feature outreach activities and strategies of various associations, organizations, and programs. Shared areas of interest include reading skills (the problem of illiteracy) and reading motivation (the problem of aliteracy); the state of the book industry; books and technology; the union of books and media in the promotion of reading initiatives; censorship; the history of books; and the international role of the book.

The 100 organizations featured in this directory are alphabetically arranged. At the head of each entry is a block of basic data that includes the name and address of the organization; the telephone number; the name and title of person to contact for additional information; and the year in which the organization was founded. Beneath this block are four narrative sections: **What/For Whom, Examples, Publications,** and **Sources of Support.**

What/For Whom—presents an overview of the organization, describing what it is, whom it serves, and what it does for them. Descriptions are based largely on materials that were provided by the organizations and programs themselves.

Examples—focuses on those projects that illustrate the organizations's reading and book promotion activities, particularly among general audiences. This section, in most cases, is considered to be the heart of the entry in terms of the community of the book. It describes the aims and interests that, as a member of the book community, the organization or program shares with the Center for the Book.

Publications—focuses on printed materials related to reading and books.

Sources of Support—describes how the organizations are funded and serves to stimulate in readers ideas and projects they can adapt to their own organizational need and structures.

"A Few Other Resources," located after the alphabetical list, describes a number of publications, projects, and organizations that did not fit into the main list of organizations. The index covers the introduction, the directory, and "A Few Other Resources," including names of organizations, suborganizations, projects, and individuals as well as giving subject access to the information in this volume.

Organizations
and Programs

Cross-references to other organizations are given in the directory by entry number (§).

§1   ACTION

806 Connecticut Avenue, N.W.
Washington, D.C. 20525
202-634-9135
Established in 1971

What/For Whom

ACTION is the principal agency in the federal government for administering volunteer service programs. It operates through ten regional offices. Its programs are authorized by the Domestic Volunteer Service Act of 1973 as amended.

Examples

1) ACTION is a member of the Coalition for Literacy (§39).

2) Older American Volunteer Program. The department runs three programs that include literacy training: the Foster Grandparent Program, the Senior Companion Program, and the Retired Senior Volunteer Program. Of these, the Retired Senior Volunteer Program (RSVP) has the largest literacy project. RSVP provides opportunities for retired men and women, aged sixty and over, to serve on a regular basis in a variety of settings throughout their communities. Senior volunteers are part-time and do not receive stipends. They work under the auspices of an established community service organization with funding, support, and technical assistance provided by ACTION and the local community. For further information, contact Janet Farbstein, Program Specialist, 202-634-9353.

3) Volunteers in Service to America (VISTA). VISTA added literacy training to its program when Congress passed a series of amendments to the legislation in May 1984. To supplement ongoing VISTA literacy activities, Congress appropriated additional funds in 1987 for the establishment of VISTA Literacy Corps. VISTA volunteers work in recruitment, training, and retention of both tutors and students in low income communities with relatively high illiteracy rates. Priority is given to currently unserved or underserved populations. For further information, contact Diana London, Chief, 202-634-9424.

4) Program Demonstration and Development. Through this office, ACTION funds demonstration grants related to volunteerism. Recent grants have supported projects concerned with illegal drug use prevention, foster care, youth, farm families in crisis, and illiteracy. The focus is on innovative ways of addressing social problems using volunteers. Demonstration projects that are funded must have the potential for widespread use through replication. A recent literacy grant, for example, funded the development of films to teach literacy trainers in rural areas. For more information, contact Phil McLaurin, Demonstration Program Officer, 202-634-9757.

Source of Support

Federal government.

17

§2

Action for Children's Television (ACT)

20 University Road
Cambridge, Massachusetts 02138
617-876-6620
Peggy Charren, President
Established in 1968

What/For Whom

Action for Children's Television is a national nonprofit child advocacy group that works to encourage diversity in children's television programming and to eliminate abuses in advertising aimed at children. ACT initiates legal reform and promotes public awareness of issues relating to children's television through public education campaigns, publications, awards, national conferences, and speaking engagements. ACT's efforts to improve broadcasting practices related to children include filing petitions with the Federal Trade Commission, testifying before the Congress in favor of legislation (e.g., the Children's Television Education Act), working with the television industry itself, and cooperating with professional associations concerned with children's welfare. Awards from ACT highlight achievements in children's television. ACT resource books provide information on special subjects in children's programming, including the arts, consumerism, stereotyping, children who are disabled, role models, and the sciences. In 1986, ACT gave its resource library to Gutman Library at Harvard University's School of Education. It is now helping Harvard raise funds to house and organize the collection.

Examples

1) In 1980, ACT and the Center for the Book in the Library of Congress (§32) cosponsored the symposium "Broadcasting Books to Young Audiences," in which authors, editors, producers, broadcasters, and librarians explored ways of developing more children's television programming based on books. As a result of the conference, ACT asked publishers of children's books to choose books they have published that would make good television programs. The suggestions were published by ACT as *Editors' Choice: A Look at Books for Children's TV* (1982).

2) ACT's 1986 publication *Television, Children, and the Constitutional Bicentennial* was designed to stimulate in children and adolescents high quality television programming concerning the history and significance of the Constitution.

3) The booklet *Children and Television News* was the starting point of ACT's 1987 campaign to promote awareness of how the news can be used to benefit young audiences and to encourage broadcasters to produce programs to meet the needs of children.

4) In 1987, ACT cosponsored a conference with WGBH-TV in Boston on the future of children's television.

Publications   Many bibliographies, resource books, and handbooks.

Sources of Support   Membership contributions; gifts from foundations, corporations, and public agencies.

---

§3   Adult Performance Level Project (APL)

College of Education
Education Building, Suite 244
University of Texas at Austin
Austin, Texas 78712
512-471-4285
Oscar G. Mink, *Director*
Established in 1971

What/For Whom   "Adult Performance Level" is an educational concept that emerged from research begun in 1971 at the University of Texas with funding from the U.S. Department of Health, Education, and Welfare. The objectives of the research project were to describe adult functional literacy in pragmatic, behavioral terms and to develop instruments for measuring functional competency. Other products of the research included a skills curriculum to teach functional competency and a competency-based high school diploma program that awards a regular diploma for the demonstration of these skills. APL offers technical assistance and training to literacy organizations in the establishment, administration, and evaluation of this Competency-Based Curriculum and High School Diploma (CBHSD) Program.

Publications   *Final Report: The Adult Performance Level Study,* published in 1977, presents the findings of the study funded by the Department of Health, Education, and Welfare. APL's instructional system is decribed in *The APL Series: Coping in Today's Society,* published by Harcourt Brace Jovanovich

Sources of Support   Publications, training and consulting fees, royalties, and administrative support from the University of Texas.

§4 American Antiquarian Society (AAS)

185 Salisbury Street
Worcester, Massachusetts 01609-1634
617-755-5221
Marcus A. McCorison, *Director and Librarian*
Established in 1812

What/For Whom

The American Antiquarian Society is an important research library that specializes in American history to 1877. The AAS holds approximately two-thirds of the items known to have been printed in this country between 1640 and 1821, as well as the most useful source materials and reference works printed since that period. The collections serve a worldwide community of students, teachers, historians, bibliographers, genealogists, and authors whose work at the society reaches a broad audience through textbooks, biographies, historical novels, newspapers, periodicals, plays, films, and library programs. In addition, the society's own library staff prepares scholarly publications, for example, a history of printing in American newspapers and the standard work on Paul Revere's engravings. AAS also awards fellowships and sponsors seminars, public lectures, and academic programs.

Examples

1) The Program in the History of the Book in American Culture, established in 1983, is aimed at stimulating research and education in this interdisciplinary field. The program sponsors scholarly activities, including annual lectures, workshops, conferences, publications, and residential fellowships. In 1987, the program cosponsored a two-day conference with the Center for the Book of the Library of Congress (§32) on "Teaching the History of the Book: Methods and Concepts." The conference was concerned with the question of incorporating the history of the book into the liberal arts curriculum and into the curriculum of professional schools such as those in library and information science and journalism.

2) The third seminar (1988) in the History of the Book in American Culture examined the theme "The Politics of Writing, Reading, and Publishing in Nineteenth-Century America." The second seminar (1986) focused on the theme "The American Common Reader: Printing, Entrepreneurship, and Cultural Change, 1759-1840."

Publications

The Newsletter of the AAS, monthly; *The Book: The Newsletter of the Program in the History of the Book in America Culture*, three times a year; and *Proceedings of the American Antiquarian Society*, twice a year. *Teaching the History of the Book*, proceedings of the 1987 conference, also contains two of the papers given and the syllabi distributed at the conference.

Sources of Support

Private support and federal grants.

§5

American Association for Adult and Continuing Education (AAACE)

1112 Sixteenth Street, N.W., Suite 420
Washington, D.C. 20036
202-463-6333
Judith A. Koloski, *Executive Director*
Established in 1982

What/For Whom

AAACE is a private, nonprofit national service organization for professionals in the fields of adult and continuing education. Services include conferences, advocacy, dissemination of information, research, and staff development and training. The association offers programs in literacy, adult basic education, and English as a second language, as well as in adult and continuing education. Staff development and training services focus especially on training teachers how to teach adults to read and think critically. The association's Division of State, Local, and Institutional Management contains the National Council of State Directors of Adult Education (NCSDAE), which, through a network of government-funded literacy programs in every state, provides professional classroom instruction to over two million adults in need of basic reading skills. The Division of State, Local, and Institutional Management also includes the Administrators of Adult Education, which provides similar services at the local level.

Examples

1) AAACE and NCSDAE are members of the Coalition for Literacy (§39).

2) Life Skills Program. The program includes the Commission on Adult Basic Education, which focuses on literacy and English as a second language.

3) To mark National Adult and Continuing Education Week in 1988, AACE cosponsored a professional development workshop via satellite with USA Today and PBS. The event, entitled "Teaching Today's Adults: Focus on Careers," featured adult education teachers as they taught reading, writing, critical thinking, and career development skills to adult students in a wide variety of settings.

Publications

Online with Adult and Continuing Educators, a newsletter; two journals, *Lifelong Learning* and *Adult Education Quarterly;* and a variety of pamphlets and books on current issues in adult and continuing education.

Sources of Support

Membership dues, conferences, publications, and foundation grants.

§6   American Association of Retired Persons (AARP)

1909 K Street, N.W.
Washington, D.C. 20049
202-872-4700
Established in 1958

What/For Whom

AARP is the oldest and largest service and advocacy organization of older Americans, representing roughly one-fourth of all Americans over the age fifty-five. Its purpose is to improve the quality of life for older Americans through efforts in such areas as age discrimination, health care, consumer affairs, crime prevention, tax assistance, research on aging, and adult continuing education. AARP legislative specialists lobby for the interests of older Americans at both state and federal levels. Membership is open to anyone aged fifty or older, whether retired or not.

Examples

1) Institute of Lifetime Learning. The institute is AARP's continuing education service. It promotes learning opportunities for older people, helps them prepare for new careers, and promotes their involvement in media and new technologies. As a resource center on lifetime learning and aging, it publishes materials related to education for older people and helps them establish discussion groups. The institute also conducts surveys, initiates workshops, and provides technical assistance to organizations interested in developing educational programs for older people. For further information contact Sandra W. Sweeney, Director, Institute of Lifetime Learning. 202-662-4895.

2) The AARP and the American Newspaper Publishers Association (ANPA) Foundation (§13) produced a newspaper advertisement and poster to encourage and direct older Americans to combat illiteracy by volunteering their time and talent to help younger people.

Publications

A bimonthly magazine, *Modern Maturity;* the monthly *AARP News Bulletin;* brochures; and handbooks.

Sources of Support

Membership dues, magazine subscriptions, investments, and sale of advertising.

§7

American Booksellers Association (ABA)

137 West Twenty-fifth Street
New York, New York 10001
212-463-8450
Bernard Rath, *Executive Director*
Established in 1900

What/For Whom

The American Booksellers Association's purpose is "to define and strengthen the position of the book retailer in the book distribution chain." Its members are individuals and firms engaged in the retail sale of books in the United States. Association activities include promoting the retail sale of books, fostering sound bookseller-publisher relations, aiding booksellers in the encouragement of reading at all age levels, and representing the interests of booksellers on legal issues, such as First Amendment concerns and alleged unfair trade practices. The ABA also sponsors national conferences, as well as educational seminars and workshops on bookselling for its membership.

Examples

1) The ABA will use "The Year of the Young Reader" as the theme of its 1989 annual conference. The ABA used the Center for the Book's "Year of the Reader" theme during its 1987 annual conference. Celebrity speakers were asked to preface their remarks with anecdotes about books that made a difference in their lives. "The Year of the Reader: Freedom to Read" was the focus of a panel discussion on the First Amendment. The "Year of the Reader" theme was also used in different sectors of the book industry, with offerings ranging from an ABA merchandising kit to bookbags and bookmarks.

2) In 1987, ABA board and staff members presented books to the President for the White House Family Library.

3) The Media Coalition. The coalition, consisting of trade associations of publishers, distributors, and retailers in the print media, combats attempts to censor the sale of certain books and periodicals.

4) Banned Books Week is cosponsored annually each September by the ABA, the American Library Association (§12), the National Association of College Stores (§66), the Association of American Publishers (§19), and the American Society of Journalists and Authors. Its goal is to highlight books that have been banned, thus attracting media attention to threats against the First Amendment and the importance of the freedom to read. Several state affiliates of the Center for the Book (§32) sponsor Banned Books Week programs.

Publications

ABA Newswire is a comprehensive weekly newsletter for booksellers that lists forthcoming publicity about books and authors.

It contains succinct information about TV and radio appearances, lectures, articles, and book reviews, as well as major advertising and promotional offers. *American Bookseller,* a monthly magazine of news and features of interest to booksellers, includes a section on "Books & the Media," providing summaries of current and upcoming movies and television programs that have a connection to books. *Basic Book List,* a periodically revised list of staple hardbound and paperback titles recommended as a nucleus for a bookstore's basic stock, reflects actual sales records in bookstores across the country. The fourth edition of *A Manual on Bookselling: How to Open and Run a Bookstore* was published in 1987.

Sources of Support   Membership dues and trade exhibits.

---

§8   American Council of Learned Societies (ACLS)

228 East Forty-fifth Street, 16th Floor
New York, New York 10017
212-697-1505
Stanley N. Katz, *President*
Established in 1919

What/For Whom   The American Council of Learned Societies is a federation of national organizations concerned with the humanities and the humanistic elements of the social sciences. Its forty-five members are scholarly associations in areas of language, literature, philosophy, religion, history, the arts, law, political science, sociology, and psychology. ACLS promotes the humanities through fellowships, grants-in-aid, and travel and exchange awards to scholars; investigations into the needs of humanistic scholarship; and cooperation both nationally and internationally with other organizations.

Examples   1) With the Social Science Research Council, ACLS sponsors the International Research and Exchanges Board, which is responsible for several scholarly exchange programs with Eastern European countries. The aim is to enable U.S. scholars to study in Eastern Europe and the USSR and to enable Eastern scholars to study in the United States.

2) The ACLS has directed the preparation of several large, vital reference works, the *Dictionary of American Biography,* the *Dictionary of Scientific Biography,* and the *Dictionary of the Middle Ages.* In 1987, ACLS signed a contract with Oxford University Press to produce a major new reference work tentatively entitled *American National Biography (ANB),* which will be a successor of the earlier *Dictionary of American Biography.*

3) From 1984 to 1987, ACLS sponsored an Office of Scholarly Communication and Technology which studied and provided information about methods of scholarly communication.

Publications

A quarterly newsletter, an annual report, and occasional pamphlets.

Sources of Support

Grants from foundations, the National Endowment for the Humanities (§75), and corporations; fees from members and a number of colleges and universities that are associate members.

§9 American Federation of Labor-Congress of Industrial Organizations (AFL-CIO)

815 Sixteenth Street, N.W.
Washington, D.C. 20006
202-637-5144
Jim Auerbach, *AFL-CIO Department of Education*
Established in 1955

What/For Whom

The American Federation of Labor-Congress of Industrial Organizations (AFL-CIO) represents American labor in world affairs through participation in international labor bodies. It coordinates activities such as community services, political education, and voter education. Sometimes referred to as a "union of unions," the AFL-CIO is a voluntary federation of roughly one hundred national and international unions representing thousands of local unions.

The AFL-CIO actively promotes literacy and basic skill training through its own Department of Education. The federation is especially concerned with displaced and laid-off workers who are unable to qualify for retraining programs. Thus, it emphasizes literacy and basic education programs linked to retraining and employment.

Examples

1) AFL-CIO/American Library Association (ALA) Joint Committee on Library Service to Labor Groups. The joint committee was established with the American Library Association (§12) to foster closer cooperation between librarians and labor organizations. It promotes awareness of common interests among librarians and labor educators and encourages wider and more intensive patronage of libraries by members of the labor community and their families. In recent years, the joint committee has published a bibliography for librarians and others to use in building a library collection about labor, as well as bibliographies on workplace health and safety and on women workers. The committee also gives programs and sponsors film

and materials exhibits at ALA conferences. One recent program, for example, focused on ways in which libraries can serve the unemployed during recession and recovery. The joint committee actively supports the ALA's National Library Week.

2) In 1981, the ALA established the John Sessions Memorial Award to recognize a library or library system that works effectively with the labor community. John Sessions, Assistant Director of the AFL-CIO Department of Education, was very active on the AFL-CIO Joint Committee on Library Service.

3) Many local union programs address the problem of literacy. Eight unions in the New York City area have formed the Consortium for Workplace Literacy. With an estimated 50 percent of its combined workers and families in need of literacy skills, the consortium has used public funds appropriated for adult education to build a program based on two premises: the importance of providing education to help workers maintain current jobs or retrain for new ones before job loss and the effectiveness of learning in a functional context with curricula built around the occupational themes and life experiences of the various union memberships. The consortium's activities now make up one-third of the adult education classes provided by the New York City Board of Education.

Publications

Education Update, bimonthly reports prepared by the AFL-CIO Department of Education on labor conferences, workshops, new publications, and other resources; various pamphlets and bibliographies.

Source of Support

Union dues.

§10 American Institute of Graphic Arts (AIGA)

1059 Third Avenue
New York, New York 10021
212-752-0813
Caroline Hightower, *Director*
Nathan Gluck, *Competition Coordinator*
Established in 1914

What/For Whom

The American Institute of Graphic Arts is a national nonprofit organization of graphic design and graphic arts professionals. It conducts an interrelated program of competitions, exhibitions, publications, professional seminars, education activities, and projects in the public interest in order to promote excellence in the graphic design profession. Institute members are involved in the design and production of books, magazines, and periodicals as well as corporate, environmental, and promotional graphics.

Examples

1) The biennial AIGA conference is the only national conference devoted exclusively to the graphic arts.

2) Competition for the annual Book Show makes acceptance one of the most prestigious awards for book design. Books accepted for the show appear in *AIGA Graphic Design USA.*

3) AIGA annually awards medals for distinguished achievement in the graphic arts, including book design.

Publications

AIGA Journal of Graphic Design, a quarterly which includes information on trends, professional practices, and individuals in the field, past and present; *Graphic Design USA,* an annual recording the work selected in the year's national competitions for exhibition and the portfolios of the Medalist and Leadership Design recipients; *AIGA Membership Directory;* and other professional publications.

Sources of Support

Membership dues, corporate sponsors, subscriptions, sale of publications, and federal grants (for the national conference).

---

§11 American International Book Development Council (AIBDC)

4000 Albemarle Street, N.W.
Washington, D.C. 20006
202-362-8131
William Childs, *Executive Director*
Established in 1985

What/For Whom

The American International Book Development Council was established as an arm of the Helen Dwight Reid Educational Foundation in response to problems at home and abroad that create and perpetuate a gap between book needs and availability. The council develops and undertakes projects aimed at enhancing book access at home and abroad and facilitates the exchange of information among readers, in particular the students, scholars, educators, and scientists needing a global exchange of ideas on common concerns. In addressing the needs of this literate community, the council works with individuals and groups in the private publishing industry, the international library and book donation programs, education institutions, and governmental agencies, as well as regional and worldwide organizations. The council works in seven areas to remove obstacles that impede the flow of published materials into and from the United States: bibliographic dissemination, acquisition information, education in publishing, copyright, country and regional profiles, and professional publishing services.

Examples

1) The council is developing a guide titled "How to Buy American Books," a basic, practical approach to the entire U.S. export community for foreign book importers. The guide will be based on responses to a questionnaire the council has sent out to 600 firms in book publishing and allied industries.

2) The council is participating in a project initiated by the Canadian Organization for the Development of Education (§28), the development and production of *A Directory of American Donated Book Programs.*

3) American Access to Foreign Literature is another major council program which seeks the cooperation of librarians, booksellers, and book importers in the United States to supplement information gathered from foreign book exporters and publishers.

Publications

Book Access Report, a newsletter; *American Books Abroad; U.S.-Soviet Book Publishing Relations: Cultural Accord or Discord?;* and other monographs.

Sources of Support

Contributions from individuals and corporations; grants from nonprofit organizations, foundations, and governmental bodies.

---

§12 American Library Association (ALA)

50 East Huron Street
Chicago, Illinois 60611
312-944-6780
Peggy Barber, *Associate Executive Director for Communication Services*
Established in 1876

What/For Whom

The American Library Association is the oldest and largest library association in the world. In addition to librarians, its forty-seven thousand members include library educators and researchers, publishers, and the general public. Its members represent all types of libraries: public, school, academic, and special—the libraries that serve governments, businesses, and armed services, hospitals, prisons, and other institutions. ALA's goals include improving library services, promoting reading, promoting the public awareness of libraries, increasing the accessibility of information, protecting the right to read, and monitoring and improving the education of librarians.

Examples

1) ALA promotes reading and the use of libraries through public service announcements in national media, news articles, posters, publicity guides for librarians, and public relations campaigns, often in close cooperation with other organizations.

2) National Library Week, held in April, is ALA's biggest annual promotion effort. Each year, ALA's Public Information Office selects a theme, prepares promotional television and radio spots, posters, and other materials, and creates a kit for distribution to librarians throughout the United States. Some effort goes toward national publicity, but the great emphasis is on enabling local libraries of all kinds to enlist local support in promoting libraries and library use. National Library Week Partners is an organization of about sixty-three associations, organizations, and businesses that support National Library Week. The 1987 theme for National Library Week was "Take Time to Read," which saluted the Year of the Reader proclaimed by the Center for the Book in the Library of Congress (§32). The 1988 theme was "The Card with a Charge—Use Your Library."

3) ALA's Year of the Reader celebration also included a "Reader's Poll" distributed by more then 750 libraries. Some sixty-two thousand readers, including Ann Landers, Julian Bond, and President Reagan, cast their votes in such categories as funniest, scariest, and best book or favorite place to read. For "1989—The Year of the Young Reader," also a Center for the Book initiative, ALA is using the Year of the Young Reader logo on bookmarks, banners, bookbags, the 1989 Caldecott calendar, and the Caldecott and Newbery lists. A "Nation of Young Readers" poster has also been produced.

4) National Library Card Campaign. In 1987, ALA and the National Commission on Libraries and Information Science (§70), with the assistance of the U.S. Department of Education, launched a national campaign to encourage every child in America to have a library card and use it. The campaign has become an annual event.

5) The Office for Intellectual Freedom coordinates ALA programs in the areas of intellectual freedom and censorship. ALA cosponsors an annual Banned Books Week with the American Booksellers Association (§7), the American Society of Journalists and Authors, the Association of American Publishers (§19), and the National Association of College Stores (§66). ALA also founded the Freedom to Read Foundation (§46), which supplies legal support to librarians and others engaged in First Amendment-related struggles.

6) The Office for Library Outreach Services trains resource personnel who in turn train others in the library field to develop and conduct literacy programs. Management of the Coalition for Literacy (§39) is a function of this office. For further information, contact Sibyl Moses, Director, 800–545-2433.

7) The American Association of School Librarians received a grant from the Houghton Mifflin Company to develop, in cooperation with the Association for Library Service to Children, "Librarian Involvement in the Reading Process: A Demonstration Project." Both associations are divisions of ALA.

8) Awards. The Association for Library Service to Children annually awards the Newbery Medal for the year's most distinguished contribution to American literature for children and the Caldecott Medal for the year's most distinguished picture book for children. The Public Library Association sponsors the Advancement of Literacy Award to an American publisher or bookseller for work advancing literacy; and the American Library Trustee Association sponsors the Literacy Award for contributions toward fighting illiteracy. ALA makes many other awards, most for improvements and progress in librarianship.

9) The Resources and Technical Service Division is deeply involved in efforts to study and encourage the preservation of books and other library materials.

10) ALA administers the Library/Book Fellows program made possible by a grant from the U.S. Information Agency (§96).

Publications

American Libraries is a monthly membership magazine that covers the breadth of ALA's interests with news and feature articles. Each of ALA's divisions publishes a journal and many publish newsletters. *Booklist* provides prepublication book reviews for public libraries; *Choice* does the same for college and university libraries. ALA publishes many books in library management and recently published three titles dealing with literacy: *Library Materials in Service to the New Reader, Libraries and Literacy: A Planning Manual,* and *Reading Instruction for the Adult Illiterate.* Booklists, many of them pamphlets, are available from ALA. These are selective lists of readings, some arranged by topic, others by audience (adults, young adults, children). Some are not only selective but the results of awards selections. Posters promoting libraries, books, and reading are also available from ALA.

Sources of Support

Membership fees, endowment income, conference proceeds, grants from foundations and government agencies.

§13

American Newspaper Publishers Association Foundation (ANPA Foundation)

The Newspaper Center
Box 17407
Dulles International Airport
Washington, D.C. 20041
703-648-1000
Judith D. Hines, *Executive Vice President*
Carolyn Ebel Chandler, *Manager/Literacy Programs*
Established in 1961

What/For Whom

The American Newspaper Publishers Association Foundation is a public nonprofit educational foundation devoted to strengthening the press in America. Its programs encompass three principal goals: advancing professionalism in the press through support for journalism education; fostering public understanding of a free press; and cultivating future newspaper readers.

The Newspaper in Education (NIE) program, a major ANPA service, aids parents and educators in teaching young people the fundamentals of reading and of informed citizenship. The NIE program is a cooperative effort between daily newspapers and thousands of U.S. and Canadian schools that use the newspapers to teach a variety of subjects: social studies, math, history, and English, as well as reading. ANPA is a coordinating agency for these local programs. It develops and distributes materials, sponsors conferences for developing NIE programs, and advises individual schools and newspapers. The newspapers themselves provide copies of their papers to schools at discount prices, offer curriculum materials and teacher training, and generally help schools develop newspaper use for student learning.

As a supporter of freedom of the press, the ANPA Foundation is a sponsoring member of the First Amendment Congress, an organization composed of all major professional journalism organizations and committed to enhancing America's awareness of the importance of freedom of expression in a democratic society. ANPA acts as the administrative service arm of the congress and publishes its newsletter. It also awards grants to support groups such as the Reporters Committee for Freedom of the Press and the World Press Freedom Committee.

Examples

1) National NIE Week. Annually cosponsored by the International Reading Association (§57) and the ANPA Foundation in cooperation with state and regional press associations, National

Newspaper in Education Week promotes the teaching of reading in the classroom through the use of newspapers.

2) Family Focus: Reading and Learning Together. This program, launched in fall 1988, is cosponsored by the ANPA Foundation, the International Reading Association (§57), the National PTA (§77), and the National Association of Elementary School Principals. The program is designed to help parents learn new ways of working with their children to foster good reading habits and improved reading skills, emphasizing newspapers as effective teaching tools for children of all ages.

3) Press to Read. This three-year newspaper literacy campaign was started in 1986 to support the efforts of public and private adult literacy programs. To help newspapers begin literacy efforts, ANPA Foundation produced *Newspapers Meet the Challenge* (a handbook), *Showcase of Newspaper Literacy* (a review of some newspaper projects across the country), and a twenty-minute slide/video program about illiteracy. Literacy Creators workshops have also been conducted. The campaign includes an outreach program aimed at developing cooperative projects with major educational organizations.

4) National Newspaper Literacy Day. ANPA Foundation's involvement in National Newspaper Literacy Day in 1988 included a national literacy symposium "Who's Learning to Read and How Do We Know?" held in cooperation with the International Reading Association (§57), the U. S. Department of Education (§95), and other major adult literacy programs. The purpose was to assess adult students' progress in instructional programs. A national newspaper readathon, cosponsored with the International Reading Association, encouraged newspapers to initiate readathons in cooperation with community groups.

5) ANPA Foundation will sponsor the First Annual Newspaper Adult Literacy Conference in Denver, July 9-11, 1989. Sessions will cover such topics as readership/circulation and illiteracy, worksite literacy, easy-read copy, and intergenerational issues.

Publications

NIE publications include teacher guides and curriculum materials to advance the classroom use of newspapers; the booklet "Using the Newspaper to Teach Gifted Students"; *Update NIE*, a monthly report; and *Press to Read*, the literacy newsletter issued five times during the year to newspaper publishers, editors, and others interested in literacy news.

Sources of Support

NIE programs and publications income; sale of promotional material; and proceeds from the foundation's endowment fund, which is supported by contributions from newspapers, newspaper organizations, and individuals in the newspaper business.

§14 American Printing History Association (APHA)

P. O. Box 4922, Grand Central Station
New York, New York 10163
212-673-8770
Renee Weber, *Executive Secretary*
Founded in 1974

What/For Whom

The American Printing History Association is a nonprofit membership organization founded to encourage the study of printing history and its related arts and skills, including calligraphy, typefounding, papermaking, bookbinding, illustration, and publishing. APHA has members from throughout the book world, for example, book collectors, librarians, printers, editors, private press owners, and historians. It sponsors exhibits and conferences, compiles statistics, conducts censuses of artifacts and archives, and presents an annual award for an outstanding contribution to printing history. APHA both coordinates projects in the history of printing and encourages the preservation of the artifacts of the printing trade by museums.

Example

The fall conferences of APHA have each focused on a topic in printing history. The 1987 conference theme was "Government Printing in the Western Hemisphere: Technology, Design, Politics." The 1988 conference, the first to be held outside New York, took place in Philadelphia and focused on the "Book Arts in Philadelphia, 1790-1830." The 1989 conference, commemorating the beginning of printing in the United States, will be held in Cambridge, Massachusetts, where printing began 350 years ago.

Publications

The APHA Letter is a bimonthly newsletter covering the full range of APHA's interests including news, listings of lectures and exhibitions, book reviews, and notices of printing equipment for sale. *Printing History* is a semiannual scholarly journal with articles reflecting the broad range of printing history, as well as reviews and other features.

Sources of Support

Membership dues, contributions, and sale of publications.

§15

American Reading Council, Ltd.

45 John Street
Room 908
New York, New York 10038
212-619-6044
Julia Reed Palmer, *President*
Established in 1976

What/For Whom

The American Reading Council promotes the development of literacy through changes in educational policy. It also disseminates information about effective literacy projects, administers demonstration programs, and assists others in initiating and improving their own literacy services. The council focuses on young children and their parents and teachers, although some literacy work is also done with adults who are illiterate. Approaches advocated by the council include: quality elementary school libraries, quality childhood education, community involvement in education programs, and literature-based curricula for children and adults.

Examples

1) The Friendly Place/El Sitio Simpatico. The centerpiece of this East Harlem family learning center is a community-based paperback library of thirty thousand titles and a bookstore that carries low-cost books. Preschoolers and their parents are introduced to books through educational play groups, a parenting section in the library, and a sales section of preschool books. There are also satellite libraries in nearby preschool and senior citizen centers. The Friendly Place has recently become an autonomous community-based agency.

2) Mothers' Reading Program. The focus of this program has been expanded by creating an intergenerational model of family literacy by instituting classes for illiterate mothers of Head Start children. Mothers and children both learn to read from their own words written down and from exposure to literature.

3) Open Sesame. This model reading curriculum offers youngsters in Head Start and public school kindergarten the opportunity to learn to read in an unpressured pleasurable way through the use of language experience and immersion in children's literature.

4) Exemplary Library Program. During the 1987-88 school year, the American Reading Council developed a pilot program that brought selected New York City school systems together with the public library system to provide exemplary library services for children.

5) With help from a major grant from the Reader's Digest Foundation, the council has begun a national dissemination of the community-based literacy education model it developed for children and adults in low-income sections of New York.

Publications

Open Doors: A Decade of Educating Those at Risk (July 1987) reviews the history and achievements of the council.

Sources of Support

Contributions from foundations, corporations, and individuals.

---

§16

Antiquarian Booksellers Association of America (ABAA)

50 Rockefeller Plaza
New York, New York 10020
212-757-9395
Janice M. Farina, *Administrative Assistant*
Founded in 1949

What/For Whom

The Antiquarian Booksellers Association of America was founded to encourage interest in rare books and manuscripts and to maintain the highest standards in antiquarian book trade in the United States. Its members are dealers in rare and out-of-print books. ABAA promotes exhibitions of books and related materials and offers courses and lectures on subjects of interest to book collectors. The association comments on proposed legislation relevant to its members, maintains relations with other organizations concerned with rare books, and sets guidelines for professional conduct for dealers. It also maintains an Antiquarian Booksellers' Benevolent Fund.

Publications

The Professional Rare Bookseller, a journal whose publication is currently suspended, provides articles, news of the trade, and news of the ABAA. The association also publishes a directory of its members and a pamphlet, *Guidelines for the Antiquarian Booksellers Association of America,* which concerns professional ethics.

Source of Support

Membership fees.

§17

Assault on Illiteracy Program (AOIP)

410 Central Park West (PH-C)
New York, New York 10025
212-967-4008
Emille Smith, *National Coordinator*
Established in 1980

What/For Whom

AOIP, a volunteer community-building coalition of more than ninety national black-led organizations linked through a national network of 120 black-oriented newspapers, focuses on complementing and supplementing the role of teachers and tutors in overcoming illiteracy among blacks and other disadvantaged minorities. Because AOIP believes that illiteracy among blacks is the product of social, economic, and psychological damage caused by racial inequality, participating organizations pursue a two-pronged campaign that includes both literacy tutoring and "community-building." Its mission is to reach people who do not care about literacy because they do not see that it can make much difference in their lives. AOIP believes that the sense of worthlessness and despair that grows from severely deprived environmental conditions is a root cause of illiteracy and cannot be separated from the race-related realities that create such conditions.

Community-building counters low self-esteem by focusing on the local achievements of black businesses, institutions, and professionals, as reported in AOIP-participating newspapers. AOIP develops public education materials for use in various media and develops and evaluates technical material used by students and teachers. These motivational and instructional materials lead users to look toward a better life and instill pride, a sense of self-worth, and a can-do attitude.

AOIP-participating organizations conduct their literacy programs in such community-based sites as neighborhood centers, housing projects, workplaces, hospitals, nursing homes, prisons, libraries, public schools, and other public facilities. On the national level, AOIP sponsors conferences and holds public and professional workshops.

Examples

1) AOIP is a member of the Coalition for Literacy (§39).

2) AOIP communicates with its network through several newspaper operations. The first is a series of AOIP-participating community newspapers primarily associated with Black Resources, Inc. (BRI), a group of publishers responsible for the founding of AOIP. If no local participating paper exists in a area where demand is great, however, AOIP will help to create a local edition of its national newspaper, *Greater News*. At the national level, AOIP's communication needs are also served by the *National Black Monitor*.

Publications

Greater News, AOIP's national newspaper; *the Advancer*, an eight-page weekly educational supplement inserted in black-oriented community newspapers; *The Missing Link*, an eighty-page manual designed to train school teachers and volunteer tutors how to inspire people to seek out learning; and other training materials.

Sources of Support

The black-owned, community-building newspapers associated with AOIP are the major sources of all AOIP funding. Not only do the newspapers print at cost and carry *the Advancer* each week, but, in addition, their publishers have committed themselves to carrying, free of charge, AOIP and all community-building news from the AOIP-participating organizations in their area. In turn, individual members of local AOIP organizations are committed to subscribe. Additional administrative and organizing support for AOIP comes from optional membership contributions by participating organizations and materials support from national corporations.

§18 Association for Community-Based Education (ACBE)

1806 Vernon Street, N.W.
Washington, D.C. 20009
202-462-6333
Christofer P. Zachariadis, *Executive Director*
Established in 1976

What/For Whom

The Association for Community-Based Education is a national membership organization of independent, community-based educational institutions. These member institutions include accredited colleges, economic development organizations, adult learning programs, literacy projects, and advocacy organizations. ACBE promotes alternative adult education programs that advance individual development and that involve community development. Typically located in low-income communities, they serve people whose needs are not being met by more established institutions.

Services to member organizations include loans and mini-grants, technical assistance, an annual conference, regional meetings, advocacy, a scholarship program, and a clearing-house to collect and disseminate information about community-based education and its needs for resources. Adult literacy services, most often in a group setting, have traditionally been part of the educational efforts of roughly half of ACBE's member groups.

37

Examples	1) ACBE is a member of the Coalition for Literacy (§39).
	2) ACBE assembled and coordinated a literacy staff training program that was made available to ACBE members and other community-based organizations in 1988.
Publications	The biweekly *CBE Report* contains information about national policies and programs, funding opportunities, workshops, conferences, publications, and successful local programs and practices. ACBE also publishes technical assistance bulletins, an annual report, an annual membership directory, conference proceedings, and special reports on programs and practices.
Sources of Support	Contributions from private foundations and corporations, membership dues, the sale of publications, and annual conference fees.

§19 Association of American Publishers, Inc. (AAP)

220 East Twenty-third Street
New York, New York 10010
212-689-8920
Nicholas A. Veliotes, *President*
Established in 1970

What/For Whom

The Association of American Publishers, Inc. represents the United States publishing industry. Its three hundred members publish the great majority of books and pamphlets sold to American schools, colleges, libraries, bookstores, and, by direct mail, homes. AAP members also publish scholarly journals and produce a range of educational materials, including maps, films, audio and video tapes, records, slides, test materials, and computer software. AAP membership thus represents a wide spectrum of publishing activity.

The goals of the association are to expand the market for books and other published works, including journals and software; to strengthen public appreciation of the importance of books to the "stability and evolution" of society's values and culture; to provide member houses with information on trade conditions, government policies and attitudes, and other matters of concern to publishers; and to provide programs that can assist members in the management and administration of their companies. Services include conferences, statistical surveys, public information, and press relations.

Examples

1) Freedom to Read Committee. The committee is concerned with protecting freedoms guaranteed by the First Amendment. It analyzes individual cases of attempted censorship and may take action in the form of legal briefs, testimony before appropriate legislative committees, or public statements and telegrams protesting any attempt to limit freedom of communication. It also sponsors public programs and issues periodic educational reports on censorship. For additional information, contact Richard P. Kleeman, Director, Freedom to Read, AAP Washington Office, 2005 Massachusetts Avenue, N.W., Washington, D.C. 20036, 202-232-3335.

2) International Freedom to Publish Committee. The committee fights for the rights of writers and publishers around the world. For example, the committee provided moral and financial support that enabled the African Writers Association to publish *Classic* magazine. In 1983, it inaugurated a campaign, "Remember the Silenced Writer," to publicize the plight of Soviet writers.

3) An Electronic Publishing Special Interest Group (EPSIG) was established in 1986 to facilitate the use of the AAP standard and serve as an information clearinghouse on the standard and related topics.

4) "I'd Rather Be Reading." In 1983, the AAP initiated this slogan as part of a promotion campaign. The Center for the Book in the Library of Congress (§32) became the cosponsor in 1984. The slogan appeared on various promotional items and is used in conjunction with major Center for the Book promotions such as the Year of the Reader and the Year of the Young Reader.

5) AAP is a cosponsor of the annual Banned Books Week.

Publications

AAP Newsletter, published about eight times a year; *AAP Monthly Report,* a news bulletin giving comprehensive coverage of association activities; and other items of interest to the industry.

Sources of Support

Membership dues, sale of publications, and proceeds from conferences.

§20 Association of American University Presses, Inc. (AAUP)

1 Park Avenue
New York, New York 10016
212-889-6040
Evan Phillips, *Executive Director*
Established in 1937

What/For Whom

AAUP is a service organization formed to help university presses do their work more economically, creatively, and effectively. Its programs include: meetings and workshops devoted to education and training, statistical research and analysis of the industry, information exchange, fund raising, and governmental, community, and institutional relations. An extensive marketing service provides cooperative programs. An annual design competition singles out the outstanding books among those published by member presses.

Example

AAUP provides a publications service for the presses by coordinating cooperative advertising space in educational publications and newspapers. In addition, the publications program also serves the library community and works with groups of librarians to issue annual bibliographies of university press books.

Publications

The Exchange, a quarterly newsletter; the annual bibliographies *University Press Books for Public Libraries* and *University Press Books for Secondary School Libraries;* and various directories.

Sources of Support

Membership dues, conferences, and publications.

§21 Association of Booksellers for Children (ABC)

175 Ash Street
St. Paul, Minnesota 55126
612-490-1805
Betty Takeuchi, *President*
Caron Chapman, *Executive Director*
Established in 1985

What/For Whom

The Association of Booksellers for Children is an organization of businesses engaged in the retail sales of children's books. ABC provides services, studies, and programs for the advancement of children's books; promotes a high standard of business methods and ethics; and encourages a fraternal spirit on a social basis among its members. Membership includes retail booksellers who are voting members and authors, illustrators, publishers, and wholesalers who are associate members.

Examples

1) ABC is a major partner with the Center for the Book in the Library of Congress (§32) in the "1989—The Year of the Young Reader" campaign.

2) In response to repeated inquiries about how to conduct a bookfair, ABC has produced a bookfair kit. Based on information collected from members, the packet includes step-by-step procedures, examples of marketing materials, and some information on cost factors.

3) Out-of-Print Books. A list of over two hundred out-of-print book titles was gathered by members and presented to publishers to be reconsidered for reprinting. Within one year, more than one hundred of those titles were being reprinted.

4) An Awards Committee is working to produce marketing materials that can be used by members to promote children's books—whether a specific title or titles about special topics.

Publications

ABC Building Blocks is a quarterly newsletter for members. It features articles, columns, association business, member information sharing, and, once a year, a directory of ABC members.

Sources of Support

Membership dues, sale of mailing lists, and contributions.

---

§22 Authors League of America, Inc., and Authors Guild, Inc.

234 West Forty-forth Street
New York, New York 10036
212-391-9198 (Authors League); 212-398-0838 (Authors Guild)
Peggy Randall *Administrator*

What/For Whom

The Authors League of America was founded in 1912 to represent the interests of authors and playwrights regarding copyright, freedom of expression, taxation, and other issues. It consists of two component organizations, the Dramatists Guild and the Authors Guild, Inc. The Authors Guild, Inc., founded in 1921, has focused on the business and professional interests of its members, who are writers of books, poetry, articles, short stories, and other literary works. The guild and the league conduct several symposia each year at which experts provide information on such subjects of interest as privacy and publicity, libel, wills and estates, taxation, copyright, editors and editing, the art of interviewing, and standards of criticism and book reviewing. The league continues to be the sole organization representing authors in ongoing programs of the Copyright Office in the Library of Congress (see §60) affecting library photocopying and other major copyright issues. In addition, the Authors League files amicus curiae briefs on behalf of writers in the Supreme Court and federal and state appellate courts; testifies before congressional and state legislative committees; and issues public statements on various First Amendment issues, among them secrecy clauses in government contracts and book banning in schools.

Examples

1) The Authors Guild and Dramatists Guild combined forces to hold a 1987 symposium in Los Angeles on writing in different media. This was the first Authors Guild meeting outside New York City and also its first joint meeting with its sister organization.

2) In 1983, the league participated with the Center for the Book in the Library of Congress (§32) in a symposium on public lending right, the notion that authors are entitled to be compensated for the multiple uses of their books in libraries.

3) In memory of Luise Marie Sillcox, executive secretary of the Authors League of America for nearly fifty years, the league and the Center for the Book in the Library of Congress (§32) have cosponsored two lectures:"The Book," by Barbara W. Tuchman, in 1979, and the "The Book Enchained,"by Harrison E. Salisbury, in 1983.

Publications

The *Authors Guild Bulletin,* various leaflets, and pamphlets.

Sources of Support

Membership dues from the Dramatists Guild and the Authors Guild; activities fees.

§23 Bibliographical Society of America

P.O. Box 397, Grand Central Station
New York, New York 10163
718-638-7957
Irene Tichenor, *Executive Secretary*
Established in 1904

What/For Whom

The Bibliographical Society of America promotes bibliographical research and issues a variety of bibliographical publications. It sponsors a fellowship program to encourage bibliographical scholarship. Specific interests include the history of book production, publication, distribution, collecting, and author bibliography. Membership is open to libraries and individuals interested in bibliographical problems and projects. The Bibliographical Society holds its annual meeting each January in New York City.

Example

A proposal for a guide to U.S. resources for printing and publishing history has been developed by the society in cooperation with the Center for the Book in the Library of Congress (§32) and the American Antiquarian Society (§4).

Publications

The quarterly journal *Papers,* a newsletter, and occasional monographs. Also, supervision of publication of the ongoing *Bibliography of American Literature.*

Sources of Support

Membership dues, foundation grants, and sale of publications.

---

§24   Book Industry Study Group, Inc. (BISG)

160 Fifth Avenue, Suite 604
New York, New York 10010
212-929-1393
Managing Agent: *SKP Associates*
Sandra K. Paul, *President*
Established in 1976

What/For Whom

The purpose of the Book Industry Study Group is to promote and support research in and about the industry. BISG is a voluntary, nonprofit research organization composed of individuals and firms from various sectors of the book industry: publishers, manufacturers, suppliers, wholesalers, retailers, librarians, and others engaged professionally in the development, production, and dissemination of books. The group began when the Book Manufacturers' Institute (§25) brought together publishers, manufacturers, and representatives of trade associations to discuss the need to improve the industry's research capability. Trade and professional associations, such as the Association of American Publishers (§19), the Association of American University Presses (§20), and the American Booksellers Association (§7), have joined in this effort to meet the book industry's research and information needs.

Examples

1) BISG prepared two major studies of industry-wide interest: *Book Distribution in the United States* (1982) and the *Consumer Research Study on Reading and Book Purchasing* (1978, updated in 1983), a study of reading and book purchasing patterns among

adults, juveniles, and older people. The *Consumer Research Study* and its update were released and discussed at the Center for the Book in the Library of Congress (§32).

2) The Book Industry System Advisory Committee (BISAC) has helped in developing voluntary standardized computer-to-computer communications formats used throughout the industry and in expanding the acceptance of the International Standard Book Number (ISBN) and the Standard Address Number (SAN) within the publishing and bookselling community.

3) The Planning Committee sponsors an annual seminar devoted to the economic outlook of the book industry and emerging trends.

Publications

BISG publishes *Book Industry Trends,* an annual statistical research report used by the industry in business planning, the quarterly *Trends Update,* and other research reports.

Sources of Support

Membership dues and sale of publications.

---

§25 Book Manufacturers' Institute, Inc. (BMI)

111 Prospect Street
Stamford, Connecticut 06901
203-324-9670
Douglas E. Horner, *Executive Vice President*
Established in 1933

What/For Whom

BMI is the leading trade association of the book manufacturing industry and its members manufacture the majority of books published by the U.S. book publishing industry each year. BMI brings together book manufacturers to deal with common concerns and also provides links between book manufacturers and publishers, suppliers, and governmental bodies. BMI conducts studies and seminars, collects statistics, and makes forecasts about the industry's future. Each year BMI conducts one fall conference and a management conference in late April.

Examples

1) Through its affiliation with the Book Industry Study Group (§24), which it helped create, BMI has developed a data information program for the industry.

2) The Government Relations Committee and Postal Committee of BMI have worked with their counterparts at the Associa-

tion of American Publishers (§19) to present the positions of their two industries to various governmental and legislative bodies.

3) With the Association of American Publishers and the National Association of State Textbook Administrators, BMI has developed nationally recognized manufacturing standards for textbooks.

Publication *Who's Who in Book Manufacturing* (1988), a membership directory.

Source of Support Membership dues.

---

§26   Bookbuilders West (BBW)

P. O. Box 883666
San Francisco, California 94188
415-653-6362
Founded in 1969

What/For Whom Bookbuilders West is a nonprofit association founded to promote and support book publishing in the thirteen western states. It sponsors a wide variety of education programs designed to inform members about advances in publishing methods and processes or to investigate technological or aesthetic problems and solutions. BBW fosters publishing excellence and public recognition through an annual book show and it encourages qualified graphic arts students in western colleges through its annual scholarship and internship programs.

Examples 1) One or more scholarships are awarded annually to deserving students in graphic arts, editorial, or marketing courses. Summer internship programs are also arranged to attract gifted young people to western book publishing.

2) The first PubForum, a three-day event featuring seminars and exhibits from suppliers, was held in 1987.

Publications *BBW Newsletter,* a bimonthly that features news and events in western book publishing, and *The Directory of Western Book Publishers and Production Services.*

Source of Support Membership dues.

§27 Business Council for Effective Literacy (BCEL)

1221 Avenue of the Americas, 35th Floor
New York, New York 10020
212-512-2415
Gail Spangenberg, *Vice President, Programs and Operations*
Established in 1983

What/For Whom

BCEL is a publicly supported foundation established to foster greater corporate awareness of adult illiteracy and to provide guidance to the business community on needs in the field and opportunities for involvement and funding. BCEL officers and staff work with literacy programs around the country, assessing activities, needs, and problems. In addition, the council makes available to the corporate community research reports, professional and technical assistance, and other information services and sponsors meetings and seminars. It also works with schools, libraries, and other organizations to help develop the additional resources needed to build higher levels of reading competency among children. Harold W. McGraw, Jr., of McGraw-Hill, Inc. founded the council with a personal contribution of one million dollars. Its Board of Directors includes heads of major corporations and leaders in education and the professions.

Example

The BCEL played an important role in encouraging a major new study released in January 1989: JUMP START: *The Federal Role in Adult Literacy,* by the Southport Institute for Policy Analysis.

Publications

A quarterly *Newsletter for the Business Community* includes information on corporate literacy activities and on national literacy projects in search of corporate sponsorship. Other publications include the *State Directory of Key Literacy Contacts, Turning Illiteracy Around: An Agenda for National Action,* a set of two BCEL monographs that assess the short- and long-term needs of the adult literacy field and give recommendations for public- and private-sector action, and *Job-related Basic Skills: A Guide for Planners of Employee Programs,* which provides employers with step-by-step guidance on how to plan and implement an effective job-related basic skills program.

Sources of Support

Individual, corporate, and foundation contributions.

§28 Canadian Organization for the Development of Education (CODE)

321 Chapel Street
Ottawa, Ontario K1N 7Z2
613-232-3569
Robert Dyck, *National Director*
Founded in 1959

What/For Whom

The Canadian Organization for the Development of Education, formerly the Overseas Book Centre, is a Canadian, nongovernmental, nonprofit organization that supports education and literacy work in the Third World. The organization ships books and reading materials free of charge in response to requests from institutions and provides funds and supplies for the production of reading materials necessary for literacy programs. CODE is concentrating its efforts on fostering partnerships in seventeen countries in Africa and the Caribbean. They are working with local advisory boards of these countries to develop long-term plans to which CODE resources are being committed.

Examples

1) CODE's book program has developed into a specialized system aimed at meeting the precise needs of its overseas partners. Annotated booklists, updated regularly on CODE's computerized inventory, are made available to overseas educators so that they may select materials appropriate to the needs of their students.

2) Large numbers of practical and technical books were purchased for the library miniseries in health and nutrition, water management and sanitation, cooperatives, and literacy training, all specifically designed for use in developing countries.

Publications

Ngoma or Talking Drum in Swahili, official newsletter published four times per year, keeps supporters informed of CODE programs of educational assistance. The third edition of *Book Network for International Development and Education Guide to Networking* was compiled to assist book donation organizations.

Sources of Support

Funding from the Canadian International Development Agency and donations.

§29   **Cartoonists Across America**

2705 East Seventh Street
Long Beach, California 90804
Philip Yeh, *Director*
213-439-4166 or 805-735-5134
Established in 1985

What/For Whom

Cartoonists Across America is a group of cartoon artists and writers who use creativity, humor, and a variety of graphic styles to demonstrate the importance of reading to the American public. Members make appearances on request at schools, community centers, bookstores, city halls, prisons, conventions and conferences, hospitals, corporations, and fund-raising events.

Examples

1) In 1987, Cartoonists Across America began painting large dinosaur murals with the slogan "Read, Avoid Extinction" all across the United States. Their goal was to paint 100 murals by the end of 1988. During the Constitution Bicentennial celebration in 1986, they drew a giant cartoon strip to call attention to the issue of literacy and the importance of the U. S. Constitution.

2) *We the Penguins,* a comic book created by Cartoonists Across America to celebrate "1987—The Year of the Reader," featured a "Read More About It" list prepared by the Center for the Book in the Library of Congress (§32).

Publications

Several comic book series to promote literacy for all ages, including the Frank the Unicorn series, trade paperback books, and other products, such as tee shirts, posters, and bumper stickers with the dinosaurs-for-literacy theme.

Sources of Support

Corporate sponsors and sale of publications and other products.

§30

Center for Applied Linguistics (CAL)

1118 Twenty-second Street, N.W.
Washington, D.C. 20037
202-429-9292
G. Richard Tucker, *President*
Established in 1959

What/For Whom

The Center for Applied Linguistics is a private, nonprofit resource organization founded to promote the application of linguistic findings to practical language problems, to conduct research, to collect, organize, and disseminate information on languages and linguistics, and to serve as an intermediary in bringing together people and institutions concerned with language problems. Established in 1959 as an autonomous program of the Modern Language Association (§64) and incorporated in 1964 as an independent organization, CAL is concerned with the need to develop effective, flexible, and economical approaches to enhance the English-language development and literacy needs of a rapidly changing American work force. CAL's constituency is composed of private and public organizations with an interest in language practice and policy, including congressional offices, news organizations, executive agencies, and state and local officials.

Examples

1) ERIC Clearinghouse on Languages and Linguistics. CAL operates this ERIC clearinghouse under a contract from the U.S. Department of Education (§95) to provide a mechanism for the collection, organization, and broad dissemination of information about diverse aspects of language and linguistics to practitioners, policymakers, researchers, and the interested public. (See also ERIC Clearinghouse on Reading and Communication Skills [§44].)

2) Meeting the literacy needs of adults and children in the United States and abroad is an important goal of CAL's application of language research to the solution of educational and social problems. Newcomers to the United States, including refugees or immigrants, and migrants are among those whose problems are given special attention. CAL conducts research, convenes conferences, generates educational materials illustrating various approaches to literacy, and evaluates reading programs and proposed reading tests, including those being considered for statewide adoption.

Publications

Since 1987, CAL has had an agreement with Prentice Hall Regents for publication and distribution of CAL titles. Titles issued in 1987 and 1988 include *Dialects and Education: Issues and Answers* and *Second Language Proficiency Assessment: Current Issues.*

Sources of Support

Federal funds, publications, and foundation donations.

§31   Center for Book Arts

626 Broadway, 5th Floor
New York, New York 10012
212-460-9768
Cathleen Gallander, *Executive Director*
Established in 1974

What/For Whom

The Center for Book Arts is a nonprofit organization whose purpose is to promote and exhibit the art of the book, both historical and contemporary. The center offers lectures, courses, workshops, and exhibitions relating to typography, hand bookbinding, papermaking, letterpress printing, and book production. Book and paper restoration, the construction of boxes and portfolios for conservation, and the history of the book are regularly taught in courses and weekend workshops. Avant-garde creativity in bookmaking is another focus of the center, which also offers printing and binding services and workshop and studio rental.

Examples

1) The center's activities for 1988 included courses in bookbinding, book restoration, hand papermaking, and letterpress printing and weekend workshops on box-making, paper-marbling, and wood engraving.

2) The Book Arts Gallery which opened in 1986, is one of the few galleries dedicated to the book arts. The center's Book Arts store features wares such as aprons, posters, catalogues, and supplies as well as book-related arts and crafts.

Publications

Book Arts Review, a quarterly, includes a national calendar of courses, lectures, and other events on the book arts and reviews of books on the same subject.

Sources of Support

Membership fees, contributions, and grants from foundations, the New York Council on the Arts, and the National Endowment for the Arts (§74).

§32 The Center for the Book in the Library of Congress

Washington, D.C. 20540
202-707-5221
John Y. Cole, *Director*
Established in 1977

What/For Whom

The Center for the Book in the Library of Congress was established by an Act of Congress, Public Law 95-129, approved on October 13, 1977. It was created "to heighten public interest in the role of books and printing in the diffusion of knowledge." Within the Library of Congress, the center is a focal point for celebrating the legacy of books and the printed word. Outside the Library, it works closely with other organizations to foster understanding of the vital role of books, reading, and libraries. It serves as a catalyst and a source of ideas—both nationally and internationally.

A partnership between the government and the private sector, the center depends on annual, tax-deductible contributions from corporations and individuals to support its projects, symposia, exhibits, and publications. Using private funds, it sponsors projects of interest to both the general public and scholars. Its major areas of activity are literacy and reading promotion, the role of books and reading in today's society, the international role of books, and the history of books.

The catalytic function of the center has expanded dramatically since 1984 with the establishment of statewide, affiliated centers for the book in seventeen states or regions of the United States (see p. 12). The purpose of each state center is to stimulate interest in books and reading and in all parts of a state's "book culture," from author through reader. Each state center develops and funds its own operations and projects and uses promotion themes developed by the Library of Congress center. When its application is approved, a state center is granted affiliate status for a period of three years.

Examples

1) "Read More About It," the CBS Television/Library of Congress book project, is a principal Center for the Book reading promotion project. Since 1979, over three hundred CBS television presentations have included a thirty-second message in which a performer mentions books suggested by the Center for the Book and sends viewers to their local libraries and bookstores to "Read More About It!"

2) "1989—The Year of the Young Reader" is a national reading-promotion theme initiated by the Center for the Book and the Children's Literature Center in the Library of Congress (§36).

3) Two major Center for the Book projects concluded in 1987 with the publication of *The History of Books: A Guide to Selected Resources in the Library of Congress* by Alice D. Schreyer, and *Books in Our Future: Perspectives and Proposals,* a 388-page volume containing the views of over a dozen prominent advisors.

4) In 1987 the International Book Committee (§54), an advisory committee to Unesco, presented a special award to the Center for the Book for its "imaginative and practical campaigns on behalf of books and reading in all their diverse aspects, which have inspired similar efforts in the United States and internationally."

Publications

Since 1978 the Center for the Book has sponsored the publication of over sixty books and pamphlets. A list is available from the center.

Sources of Support

Private contributions with administrative support from the Library of Congress.

---

§33   Center for the Study of Reading

University of Illinois
51 Gerty Drive, Room 174
Champaign, Illinois 61820
217-333-2552
Jean Osborn, *Associate Director*
Established in 1976

What/For Whom

The Center for the Study of Reading does basic and applied research on the processes that underlie reading, reading comprehension, and the acquisition of reading skills. The center also provides outreach programs to many schools around the country and maintains close ties with other research and teacher-training institutions. Bringing a variety of perspectives to bear on the study of reading, the staff at the center includes scholars in anthropology, computer science, linguistics, literature, and several branches of psychology. The center aims at forming a consensus in the American reading community and at communicating warranted conclusions about learning to read in American schools to teachers, parents, authors, publishers, public opinion leaders, and government officials. The center administers the Reading Research and Education Center (see below) established through a grant from the U.S. Department of Education (§95).

Examples	1) The Reading Research and Education Center (RREC) is one of eleven research and development centers established and supported by the U. S. Department of Education's Office of Educational Research and Improvement (see §95) to increase knowledge about education. The center's primary mission is to conduct basic and applied research activities in the teaching and learning of literacy, which will benefit practitioners and users. Focusing on higher-order literacy skills and on the reading of content texts, the center's research program addresses the acquisition of knowledge and skills, instruction in reading, text structure and testing of reading proficency, and evaluation of instruction.

2) In the past decade, the staff of the Center for the Study of Reading has made over five hundred presentations at professional and scholarly meetings and conducted over two hundred teacher workshops. During the same period, the center has produced more than 430 technical reports and distributed nearly 100,000 copies of these reports to researchers, teachers, and policymakers throughout the world.

Publications   Over 430 technical reports have been prepared and are available through the ERIC (see §95) system. The center cosponsored the publication of *Becoming a Nation of Readers,* the report of the National Academy of Education's Commission on Reading. Other books and pamphlets are also available.

Source of Support   Grants from the U. S. Department of Education (§95).

---

§34   Chicago Book Clinic

100 East Ohio Street, Suite 630
Chicago, Illinois 60611
312-951-8254
Mercedes Bailey, *President*
Anthony Cheung, *Administrative Director*
Founded in 1936

What/For Whom   The Chicago Book Clinic promotes good craftsmanship in the editing and production of books, offers courses in various aspects of publishing, and organizes seminars, lectures, and exhibitions related to publishing and publishing technology. The Book Clinic meets monthly and its interests extend to commercial, university, and small press publishing. Its annual exhibit of award-winning designs, one of the most prestigious in the nation, includes textbooks, scholarly books, and trade books for adults and children. The Chicago Book Clinic draws on a fifteen-state area and has over nine hundred members.

Examples

1) The Chicago Book Clinic is a major sponsor of the 1989 event, "Chicago, City of the Book, Celebrates the Year of the Young Reader."

2) The clinic offers introductory courses in copy editing, book design, and other production areas.

3) The biennial exhibit "Pubtech" is an extensive and well-attended show on new technologies in publishing.

Publications

Bulletin Board, a monthly, for members; the catalog of its annual exhibit of award-winning designs; and an annual membership directory.

Sources of Support

Membership fees and contributions.

---

§35 Children's Book Council, Inc. (CBC)

67 Irving Place
New York, New York 10003
212-254-2666
John Donovan, *President*
Established in 1945

What/For Whom

CBC is a nonprofit association of publishers that encourages the reading and enjoyment of children's books. Its members publish children's and young adult trade books—books for independent reading, not textbooks. CBC's best known activity is its annual sponsorship of National Children's Book Week each November. In addition, in 1984 and 1985 the council sponsored the national conference "Everychild," which featured programming and exhibits designed to increase understanding of how all the media—books, television, movies, magazines, computers, and games—educate and provide pleasure to children and young adults.

Besides preparing reading promotion materials, CBC promotes adults' understanding of children's literature and the use of trade books in child-related disciplines. Some of this programming is developed entirely by CBC; some of it through joint CBC committees with such professional organizations as the American Booksellers Association (§7), the American Library Association (§12), the International Reading Association (§57), and the National Council of Teachers of English (§72). CBC does not offer research or marketing advice, but it does make available to the public the resources of its library, including examination copies of books recently published by its members and a professional collection of interest to children's book specialists.

Examples

1) The American Booksellers Association-Children's Book Council Joint Committee annually sponsors the exhibit and catalog "Children's Books Mean Business," which brings booksellers' attention to children's books that publishers themselves select as having a special appeal.

2) The American Library Association-Children's Book Council Joint Committee developed and published a substantial revision of its listing "Suggested Symbols for Selected Lists and Review Sources for Books for Children and Young Adults in Publishers Catalogs." Typical of its ongoing work is "Books for All Ages," a series of pamphlets listing intermixed books for young readers and adults.

3) The International Reading Association-Children's Book Council Joint Committee compiles is the annual booklist "Children's Choices: Teaching with Books Children Like."

4) The National Council of Teachers of English-Children's Book Council Joint Committee is sponsoring a three-year project, a national contest on the theme "Children's Books Open Doors." The contest, launched in December 1986, is designed to recognize teachers who enrich their students' learning experiences through children's literature.

5) In November 1988, CBC held a conference on "Social Responsibility and Children's and Young Adult Literature" in observance of National Children's Book Week and as an early activity for "1989—The Year of the Young Reader," an initiative of the Center for the Book in the Library of Congress (§32).

6) "Families Reading Together" is the theme of the CBC's 1989 Year of the Young Reader observance.

Publications

The newsletter *CBC Features* (formerly *The Calendar*), published irregularly, includes information on CBC activities, articles on children's books, and listings of free and inexpensive children's book promotion material available from CBC's publisher members. CBC also administers the preparation of three annual booklists (including lists of children's books in the areas of social studies and science) and produces posters, bookmarks, and other display and promotional material created by well-known children's book illustrators and writers. For adults, the council produces miniseminars on audio cassettes, among them "Reading Black American Poetry and African Folktales" and "Reading Poetry with Children." A revised edition of the council's *Children's Book Publishers: An Illustrator's Aid* was published in 1987. Occasional reference and informational volumes include the updated bibliographic reference *Children's Books: Awards and Prizes*.

Sources of Support

Publishers' membership dues, the annual conference, and sale of materials.

§36

Children's Literature Center, Library of Congress

Washington, D.C. 20540
202-707-5535
Sybille A. Jagusch, *Chief*
Established in 1963

What/For Whom

The Children's Literature Center in the Library of Congress provides reference, research, and bibliographic assistance to those interested in the media world of the child. It also maintains professional relationships nationally and internationally with libraries, publishers, and other organizations concerned with the education and welfare of young people. Established as the Children's Book Section, it received its present name and function in 1978 when it became part of the Library's National Programs department. Because the Library of Congress is primarily a research institution, the Children's Literature Center does not serve children directly but instead concentrates on services to children's book authors and illustrators, publishers, librarians, scholars, and members of the public interested in children's books. Users may work in the center's small public reading room or in the Main Reading Room of the Library of Congress.

Specialists from the Children's Literature Center recommend books and other materials for the Library's collections, helping the Library maintain a representative record of children's culture, past and present. Through their knowledge these specialists also make these collections available to those who serve children. The Library of Congress holds approximately 300,000 children's books and related items such as maps, illustrations, and sound recordings. Most children's materials are housed in the general collections, but specialized collections can be found in the Geography and Map Division, the Music Division, the Prints and Photographs Division, and the Rare Book and Special Collections Division. The rare book collection of over 18,000 volumes, for example, is especially strong in American juvenile fiction. When appropriate, the Children's Literature Center sponsors symposia, lectures, exhibits, or film programs with other Library of Congress offices.

Examples

1) National Children's Book Week is marked each November with a lecture or symposium on children's literature. The 1988 program featured noted children's book author Katherine Paterson. In 1987, the center sponsored a symposium, "Window on Japan: Children, Books, and Television Today," celebrating children's culture in Japan.

2) "1989—The Year of the Young Reader" a Library of Congress project to encourage reading among young people, is a joint initiative of the Children's Literature Center and the Center for the Book in the Library of Congress (§32).

Publications	*Books for Children: A List of Books for Preschool through Junior High Age* is compiled and published annually. It is available for $1.00 from the Superintendent of Documents, U.S. Government Printing Office, Washington, D.C. 20402. Other publications include *Stepping Away from Tradition: Children's Books from the Twenties and Thirties,* edited by Sybille A. Jagusch, and *Hans Christian Andersen: From an Artist's Point of View,* by Erik Blegvad.

Source of Support　　Federal government with supplementary funds from the private sector.

§37　Children's Television Workshop (CTW)

1 Lincoln Plaza
New York, New York 10023
212-595-3456
Keith W. Mielke, *Vice President for Research*
Established in 1968

What/For Whom　　Children's Television Workshop is the world's largest independent producer of educational television programs. It uses mass media technologies and techniques to inform and educate children primarily outside regularly scheduled classes in school. The workshop's programs are widely available and are designed to appeal to special audiences such as minorities, the economically deprived, or those with handicapping conditions. Programs appear on Public Broadcasting System (PBS) channels.

Examples　　1) Sesame Street. Targeted for children between the ages of two and five, Sesame Street's goal is to help prepare preschool children for the transition from the home environment to the classroom by teaching basic cognitive skills such as letters and numbers and social-emotional attributes such as pride and cooperation. Emphasis has included print literacy, prereading, writing, and vocabulary. Celebrity guests have included the first American female astronaut, Sally Ride, jazz performer Cab Calloway; violinist Itzhak Perlman; and actor and singer Harry Belafonte.

2) 3-2-1 Contact. Aimed at children from eight to twelve years old, 3-2-1 Contact shows the diverse world of science and technology at work in new and interesting ways. Programs feature a company of young hosts who travel the world in search of scientific information.

3) Square One TV. Designed for eight-to-twelve year olds, Square One TV is part of a national effort to improve mathematics education. The program's goals are to promote interest

in and enthusiasm for mathematics to encourage the use of problem-solving processes to and present a broad spectrum of mathematical topics.

4) A new workshop series on reading and writing is in early development for graduates of Sesame Street.

5) CTW developed all the instructional materials for the Jell-O Desserts Reading Rocket, a reading program that seeks to imbue children with a love of reading at a crucial point in their reading development in grades two, three and four.

Publications

Children's Television Workshop publishes books for prereaders and early readers in cooperation with companies such as Random House and Western Publishing. In addition, the workshop publishes three monthly children's magazines, *Sesame Street Magazine, 3-2-1 Contact,* and *Electric Company Magazine* (Electric Company ended broadcasting in 1986), which employs a news/feature format to encourage youngsters to discover the pleasure of reading. CTW also produces records, videotapes, toys and games, clothing, and computer software, which incorporates some of the same educational values as the television programs. For adults, CTW commissions special studies of audiences not covered by standard television audience statistics and publishes bibliographies of recent writings on workshop programming and research efforts.

Sources of Support

Product-licensing royalties, sale of periodicals and records, and overseas broadcast fees. Funds for creating new educational television programs are derived from government agencies, public broadcasting sources, foundations, and private corporations.

§38 Christian Booksellers Association (CBA)

P.O. Box 200
Colorado Springs, Colorado 80901
719-576-7880
William R. Anderson, *President*
Founded in 1950

What/For Whom

The Christian Booksellers Association is a trade association of religious bookstores. The CBA monitors and compiles statistics on the religious book trade and provides services to members through its publications program, regional meetings, and an annual national convention. The CBA makes awards, provides a placement service, and has some educational activities.

Example   The 1988 CBA convention in Dallas was attended by more
                     than ten thousand people including representatives from more
                     than seventeen hundred bookstores.

Publications   *Bookstore Journal,* a monthly, *Current Christian Books,* an annual
                     directory of suppliers, and manuals useful to member
                     bookstores.

Source of Support Membership fees.

§39   Coalition for Literacy

50 East Huron Street
Chicago, Illinois 60611
312-944-6780
Toll-free literacy hotline: 800-228-8813 (Contact Literacy
Center)
Sibyl E. Moses, *Staff Liaison, American Library Association*
Established in 1981

What/For Whom   The Coalition for Literacy was founded by the American
                     Library Association (§12) to help unify efforts to increase
                     national awareness of the problem of illiteracy. Some of the
                     coalition's objectives include: providing a mechanism for regu-
                     lar communications among member organizations; stimulating,
                     reviewing, and guiding public awareness campaigns targeted to
                     particular populations or purposes; establishing policies for the
                     operation of continuous literacy information and referral serv-
                     ices; and providing a forum for the discussion of new national
                     literacy initiatives.

                     The coalition's network includes member organizations that
                     play a role nationally and locally in the delivery of literacy
                     information and services: ACTION (§1), American Association
                     for Adult and Continuing Education (§5), American Library
                     Association (§12), Association for Community-Based Education
                     (§18), Assault on Illiteracy Project (§17), Business Council for
                     Effective Literacy (§27), Contact Center, Inc., Correctional
                     Education Association, International Reading Association
                     (§57), Laubach Literacy Action (§59), Literacy Volunteers of
                     America (§61), National Advisory Council on Adult Education,
                     National Commission on Libraries and Information Science
                     (§70), National Council of State Directors of Adult Education,
                     Urban Literacy Network (§97), Project Literacy U.S. (PLUS)
                     (§83), U.S. Department of Education (§95), and U.S. Depart-
                     ment of Labor. The membership administers the coalition on
                     a rotation basis.

Examples	1) The coalition completed a three-year public service advertising campaign (1984-87) which accomplished the objectives of increasing awareness of adult literacy as a large and growing problem, motivating prospective volunteers to join the national literacy movement, and linking them to local literacy agencies and generating support from business.

2) Toll-free literacy hotline. The coalition continues to focus on the hotline as essential to support the continuing efforts to mobilize resources and recruit volunteers and students. The hotline, staffed by the Contact Literacy Center (§40), provides information on the extent of adult literacy and refers callers to local, regional, and state literacy programs. |
| **Sources of Support** | Contributions from membership organizations. |

---

§40   Contact Literacy Center

P.O. Box 81826
Lincoln, Nebraska 68501-1826
402-464-0602
Toll-free literacy hotline: 800-228-8813
CeCe Hill, *Director of Human and Literacy Services*
Established in 1978

What/For Whom	The Contact Literacy Center is a division of Contact Center, Inc., an international nonprofit organization that offers referral and follow-up services in the areas of criminal justice and human services. The Literacy Center is the information and referral clearinghouse for the Coalition for Literacy (§39), a national literacy network. Using a toll-free national hotline (staffed from 6 A.M. to midnight seven days a week), the center responds to inquiries from all over the country. The hotline provides information to three main groups. Prospective volunteer tutors receive a listing of literacy programs in their local area and information on how they can become involved. Corporate representatives receive information on how corporations can initiate or support literacy programs. Potential students who call are referred to literacy programs in their immediate area. A special cross-referral system, when authorized, enables the Contact Literacy Center to notify area literacy programs of the interest expressed by specific potential tutors, corporations, and students. Referrals can also be provided for adults and children with learning disabilities.
Examples	1) The number of inquiries to the hotline increased from 31,000 in 1985 to 186,000 in 1987 as the result of the three-year National Awareness Campaign (see §39) completed in 1987.

Project Literacy U.S. (PLUS) (§83) public service announcements have also generated a tremendous increase in the number of calls received, with an average of 20,000 calls a month coming between 11 A.M. and 2 P.M.

2) In 1986, the center introduced a new computerized system that monitors the length of calls and provides specialized information.

Publications

The Written Word, a monthly newsletter, presents articles on literacy products, programs, and activities around the country. The center also publishes informational pamphlets on, for example, literacy statistics, fund-raising for literacy programs, publicity for literacy programs, how to help your child succeed in reading, how to form a state or local literacy coalition, how to tutor without belonging to an organization, and libraries and literacy.

Sources of Support

Sale of its publications and individual, foundation, and corporate donations through the Coalition for Literacy.

§41 Cooperative Children's Book Center (CCBC)

4290 Helen C. White Hall
University of Wisconsin-Madison
600 North Park Street
Madison, Wisconsin 53706
608-263-3720
Ginny Moore Kruse, *Director*
Established in 1963

What/For Whom

The Cooperative Children's Book Center is a noncirculating examination, study, and research children's and young adult literature library for adults. The purposes of the CCBC are to provide a collection of current, retrospective, and historical children's books; to provide Wisconsin librarians, teachers, students, and others with informational and educational services based on the collection; and to support teaching, learning, and research needs related to children's and young adult literature.

CCBC receives review copies of almost all of the trade and alternative press books published in English in the United States for children and young adults. Weekly, the center staff examines the newly published books, subsequently reads many of them, and discusses the books formally or informally with other librarians and educators in Wisconsin and elsewhere in the nation. From this process, CCBC makes selections for its annual CCBC *Choices.*

Examples

1) The twenty-five-thousand-title CCBC library collection contains review copies of juvenile trade books as they are published, recommended children's trade books, historical children's books, books by Wisconsin authors and illustrators, contemporary and historical reference or bibliographic materials related to children's literature, and alternative press books for children.

2) A two-day children's literature conference is cosponsored every other year with CCBC funding units and the University of Wisconsin-Madison Division of University Outreach. The 1989 conference on "Imagination and Literature for Children and Young Adults" will celebrate the Year of the Young Reader.

Publications

CCBC Choices, an annual annotated bibliography of selected books for children and young adults; *Alternative Press Publishers of Children's Books: A Directory;* and bibliographies on selected children's literature topics.

Sources of Support

The Wisconsin Department of Public Instruction and the University of Wisconsin-Madison with support for special projects from the Friends of the CCBC, Inc.

---

§42 Council for Basic Education (CBE)

725 Fifteenth Street, N.W.
Washington, D.C. 20005
202-347-4171
Dennis Gray, *Deputy Director*
Patte Barth, *Assistant Editor*
Established in 1956

What/For Whom

The Council for Basic Education, founded by a group of distinguished academic and civic leaders, is a nationwide association of policymakers, educators, parents, and other citizens who are advocates of liberal arts dedicated to strengthening teaching and learning in all of the basic disciplines: English (including reading and literature, writing and reasoning, speaking and listening), mathematics, science, history, geography, government, foreign languages, and the arts. The council further believes that "the first priority of American schools should be a sound education in the liberal arts, not just for a favored few but for all children."

The council promotes its goals in basic education by providing information and analysis of educational research and practice;

consulting with schools, school districts, and educational organizations; public speaking; commissioning books and special reports on timely issues; and distributing other publishers' books that it considers important. The emphasis is on primary texts by authors personally engaged in their subjects, rather than textbooks, workbooks, or edited anthologies. The council is also involved in the teaching of reading in elementary schools. The council has no local or regional affiliates.

Examples

1) Action for Better City Schools. Called Project ABCs, this program focuses public attention on the characteristics of effective schools and helps urban school districts improve the academic achievement of all students.

2) Independent Study in the Humanities. The program offers fellowships for independent summer study to high school teachers of the humanities nationwide. The program was established in 1982 by the council with a grant from the Division of Education Programs of the National Endowment for the Humanities (§75).

3)Teacher Institutes. A national network of university-based institutes assists school districts in meeting the need for more qualified and certified teachers.

4) Writing to Learn Workshops. Intensive workshops train teachers of subjects other than English to use writing as an integral part of their classes.

5) Special Programs. CBE provides consulting and inservice training to school districts, community groups, and other local organizations.

Publications

Basic Education, a monthly journal; *Basic Education: Issues, Answers, and Facts,* issued quarterly, expands on subjects previously covered in *Basic Education;* numerous books, reports, and occasional papers; and a series of citizens' guides to aid parents in judging the effectiveness of their local schools.

Sources of Support

Memberships and subscriptions, sale of publications, contributions from individuals and foundations, and government grants.

§43 Council on Library Resources, Inc. (CLR)

1785 Massachusetts Avenue, N.W.
Washington, D.C. 20036
202-483-7474
Deanna Marcum, *Vice President*
Established in 1956

What/For Whom

The Council on Library Resources is a foundation that helps libraries, particularly academic and research libraries, to make use of emerging technologies to improve operating performance and expand services. CLR interests include, along with advancing technologies, the economics and management of libraries and other information systems. In addition to grants for library management and the professional education and training of librarians, grants are given in the areas of preservation, access, and bibliographic services. The council's program concentrates on academic and research libraries because of their role in collegiate instruction, their centrality to research and scholarship, and what the council regards as "their fundamental importance to society."

Examples

1) The council's involvement in preservation-related activities increased in 1986 when it created the Commission on Preservation and Access. The commission, created on the recommendation of the council's Preservation Advisory Committee, has as its initial goal to set in motion a nationwide preservation effort to capture the contents of hundreds of thousands of brittle books by microfilming or other means, and to make them permanently accessible to all who need them. The council provides administrative support to the commission, which became an independent entity on October 1, 1988. Patricia Battin is president of the commission.

2) The council sponsored the documentary film *Slow Fires: On the Preservation of the Human Record,* which focuses on the preservation of library and archive materials. The film was funded by the council, the Andrew W. Mellon Corporation, and the National Endowment for the Humanities (§75), with assistance from the Library of Congress (§60).

Publications

CLR Reports replaces *CLR Recent Developments,* which ceased publication July 1986; also reports and brochures.

Sources of Support

Funding from private foundations and the National Endowment for the Humanities

§44

ERIC Clearinghouse on Reading and Communication Skills (ERIC/RCS)

Indiana University
Smith Research Center, Suite 150
Bloomington, Indiana 47408
812-335-5847
Ellie Macfarlane, *Associate Director*
Established in 1966

What/For Whom

The ERIC Clearinghouse on Reading and Communication is one of sixteen specialized ERIC clearinghouses sponsored by universities or professional associations through contracts with the U.S. Department of Education (§95). The ERIC/RCS center specializes in reading and communication skills, including literacy and children's literature topics. Each clearinghouse collects, evaluates, abstracts, and indexes hard-to-find educational literature; conducts computer searches; commissions studies; and acts as a resource guide. Another ERIC clearinghouse, housed at the Center for Applied Linguistics (§30), specializes in languages and linguistics.

Publications

ERIC/RCS supplies information to the general ERIC (see §95) publications. In addition, ERIC/RCS prepares brief bibliographies of recently added documents that will be useful to the classroom teacher; ERIC/RCS Reports, which appear regularly in a number of journals for educators; *ERIC/RCS News Bulletins,* semiannual newsletters for communication skills educators; and Fact Sheets. In 1985, ERIC/RCS published *Writing Is Reading: 26 Ways to Connect.*

Sources of Support

Federal funds; sales of publications, computer search services, and subscriptions.

§45   Federation of State Humanities Councils

1012 Fourteenth Street, N.W., Suite 1207
Washington, D.C. 20005
202-393-5400
Jamil S. Zainaldin, *Executive Director*
Founded in 1977

What/For Whom

The Federation of State Humanities Councils, a membership association of the state humanities councils, assists and complements the state councils in achieving their common mission: the integration of the humanities into American life. The federation has three goals: to build national support for the humanities and state humanities councils; to provide technical assistance, education, and information to state humanities councils; and to serve as a link between national organizations and state humanities councils to enrich national humanities programs. The federation monitors congressional legislation, serves as an advocate for the state councils and the humanities, sponsors training workshops, promotes and develops substantive humanities programs on a national level, and sponsors an annual conference that allows state council members and participants to exchange ideas on humanities programs.

Examples

1) The federation has created a task force with the American Council of Learned Societies (§8) to strengthen public programs by learned societies and educational organizations.

2) The federation cosponsored the Modern Language Association (§64) Conference on Literacy in 1988.

3) The Betsy McCreight Award is presented to an individual for distinguished service to the public humanities and the state councils. The Helen and Martin Schwartz Award is given to a state project that meets the objective of the reconciliation between the humanities and the public for the benefit of both.

Publications

Humanities Discourse, published bimonthly, discusses national projects in the humanities as well as state council projects. *Humanities News* provides information on state council and other humanities projects and reports on topics related to state council work. Research reports, essays, and conference proceedings are also published.

Sources of Support

A grant from the National Endowment for the Humanities (§75), other federal grants, and membership dues.

§46   Freedom to Read Foundation

50 East Huron Street
Chicago, Illinois 60611
312-944-6780
Judith Krug, *Executive Director*
Established in 1969

What/For Whom

The Freedom to Read Foundation consists of librarians, lawyers, booksellers, educators, authors, publishers, and others concerned with preserving the First Amendment rights of freedom of thought and expression. The American Library Association (§12) organized the foundation to support and defend librarians whose positions are jeopardized because of their resistance to abridgments of the First Amendment and to assist in cases that may set legal precedents regarding the freedom of citizens to read. The foundation provides legal and financial assistance to authors, publishers, booksellers, librarians, teachers, students, and others who must go to court to defend this freedom. The foundation reports to the American Library Association on a regular basis on issues of censorship and freedom to read.

Example

A Freedom to Read "Honor Roll" has been created to recognize those who have played an active role in support of intellectual freedom through their defense of the First Amendment. The first awards were presented in 1988.

Publication

Freedom to Read Foundation News, published quarterly, includes articles and reprints on censorship trends, current court cases, legislative developments in Congress and at the state level, and news regarding battles against censorship by librarians and teachers.

Sources of Support

Membership dues and administrative support from the American Library Association.

§47   Friends of Libraries U.S.A. (FOLUSA)

1420 Locust Street, Apt. 13
Philadelphia, Pennsylvania 19102
215-790-1674
Sandy Dolnick, *Executive Director*
Established in 1979

What/For Whom

Friends of Libraries U.S.A. is a national organization that works to develop and support local Friends of the Library groups. Members include over sixteen hundred Friends of Library groups, individuals, libraries, and corporations. FOLUSA is an affiliate of the American Library Association (§12) and holds its meetings in conjunction with ALA's conferences.

Examples

1) Twice a year, during the annual and midwinter ALA conferences, members of FOLUSA meet to share ideas and information.

2) FOLUSA and the Center for the Book in the Library of Congress (§32) have held three forums to discuss topics of common concern. The most recent (January 1989) was on "Federal Funds for Promoting Books, Reading, and Libraries."

Publications

Friends of Libraries U.S.A. National Notebook, quarterly, offers news of other Friends activities; *Idea Bank,* quarterly, includes special offers, program ideas, and materials available for Friends; also, pamphlets and fact sheets.

Sources of Support

Membership dues, corporate support, sale of publications, and administrative support from the American Library Association.

§48 Great Books Foundation (GBF)

40 East Huron Street
Chicago, Illinois 60611
312-332-5870
Richard P. Dennis, *President*
Founded in 1947

What/For Whom

The Great Books Foundation is an independent, nonprofit organization which promotes a liberal education program for children and adults through reading and discussion of great works of literature. With over 480,000 members, GBF supports discussion groups throughout the United States and has over sixteen series of readings. Each year, GBF trains about sixteen thousand discussion leaders in two-day sessions that are held in all fifty states. Discussion groups meet every couple of weeks for adults and at various intervals for children. Until the 1970s most discussion groups met in public libraries; now, most groups meet in local schools. Titles discussed include ancient and modern classics of literature, philosophy, and other areas.

Example

The Adult Third Series includes works from Shakespeare, the New Testament, Thucydides, Chekhov, Homer, Chaucer, James, Aeschylus, Machiavelli, and Tolstoy.

Publications

GBF publishes the series of paperback books used in Great Books discussion groups.

Sources of Support

Training fees and sales of books.

§49   Guild of Book Workers

521 Fifth Avenue
New York, New York 10175
212-757-6454
Frank Mowery, *President*
Founded in 1906

What/For Whom

The Guild of Book Workers is a national organization that promotes quality in the hand book crafts: bookbinding, calligraphy, illumination, and decorative papermaking. The guild sponsors exhibitions and offers lectures, seminars, workshops, and discussion groups.

Example

The 1987 Seminar on Standards of Excellence in Hand Bookbinding featured presentations on leather rebacking and the collaboration of printers and binders on edition binding.

Publications

The Guild of Book Workers Newsletter, a bimonthly; a semiannual journal; and a membership directory.

Sources of Support

Membership and workshop fees.

§50   Home and School Institute (HSI)

Special Projects Office
1201 Sixteenth Street, N.W.
Washington, D.C. 20036
202-466-3633
Dorothy Rich, *Founder/President*
Established in 1964

What/For Whom

Home and School Institute is a nonprofit educational organization which provides curriculum and training programs to enable schools and community organizations to involve families in their children's education. The work of the institute is based on research on how children achieve and families succeed. HSI's approach provides a guided tutoring role for families which complements but does not duplicate the work of the school. The HSI curricula are used by teachers and families directly in the classroom and at home and are keyed to prevention of drug and dropout problems.

Examples

1) New Partnerships for Student Achievement, a three-year demonstration project to enhance the role of families in their children's education, is being developed in collaboration with several organizations including the Association for Library

Service to Children of the American Library Association (§12). The project, begun in 1987, creates an infrastructure of community organizations to work with their own members and with the wider community to foster the development of skills, values, and attitudes that enable children to learn everything else.

2) HSI offers accredited workshop courses and presentations which integrate current instructional methods with supportive and nonduplicative parent-involvement strategies. Workshops are brought on site to school systems, universities, and social agencies.

3) HSI conferences address issues about family life, schooling, and work in today's society. The 1985 conference, "The Family and Educational Excellence," was cosponsored with George Washington University. The 1983 conference focused on "Single-Parent Families and the Schools: Opportunity or Crisis?"

Publications

MegaSkills: The Power to Change Your Child's Life, by Dorothy Rich, provides information for families on how to teach important skills including reading; also handbooks, guides, and other tested resources.

Sources of Support

Grants from the federal government, foundations, and institutions and sale of their publications.

§51 Information Industry Association (IIA)

555 New Jersey Avenue, N.W.
Suite 800
Washington, D.C. 20001
202-639-8262
Paul G. Zurkowski, *President*
Founded in 1968

What/For Whom

The Information Industry Association is composed of for-profit information companies and information professionals. Many members are publishers of reference books and serials, and IIA has a strong interest in the electronic delivery of information. IIA's workshops, seminars, and publications introduce members to business practices and technologies that will help to identify information needs and to deliver information cost-effectively to customers.

Example

IIA holds three major conferences each year which bring together senior information executives to explore the present and future direction of the industry, exchange ideas and experiences, and learn how to take full advantage of the opportunities of the information age.

Publications

Friday Memo, a periodic newsletter; *Information Times,* a quarterly tabloid containing feature articles, news stories, information for and about members, and updates on association activities; *Information Sources,* the annual directory of member companies; the *Product Guide of Information Products and Services;* and *The Information Millennium: Alternative Futures,* a major study on the information business of the future.

Sources of Support

Membership fees and revenues from activities and publications.

---

§52 Institute for the Study of Adult Literacy

The Pennsylvania State University
College of Education
248 Calder Way, Suite 307
University Park, Pennsylvania 16801
814-863-3777
Eunice N. Askov, *Director*
Established in 1985

What/For Whom

The Institute for the Study of Adult Literacy was established to promote a coherent and systematic means, as might be found in a university research community, to respond to the problems and issues related to literacy. Three major concerns of the institute are: study and research, improvement of practice, and advocacy and leadership.

Examples

1) Through the Adult Literacy and Technology Project, the institute coordinates efforts to infuse technology into adult literacy or adult basic education programs. Among activities of the project is an annual Adult Literacy and Technology conference.

2) Computer courseware. The institute developed and evaluated computer courseware for adult beginning reading-parents and adult beginning reading-prisoners.

3) Television Inservice Series. A three-part inservice series entitled "Helping Adults to Learn" is designed for adult basic education teachers and literacy tutors.

Publications

Adult Literacy & Technology Newsletter, published quarterly, reports, and conference proceedings.

Sources of Support

Grants from corporations and state agencies and sale of publications.

§53 International Board on Books for Young People (IBBY)

Leonhardsgraben 38a
CH-4003, Basel
Switzerland
41-6125-3404
Leena Maissen, *Executive Secretary*
Founded in 1953

United States Board on Books for Young People, Inc. (USBBY)

c/o International Reading Association
800 Barksdale Road, P.O. Box 8139
Newark, Delaware 19714-8139
302-731-4218
Alida von Krogh Cutts, *Executive Secretary*
U.S. National Section of IBBY founded in 1958
USBBY formed in 1984

What/For Whom

The International Board on Books for Young People promotes international understanding through children's books. It encourages high standards for children's books, translations of children's books, the establishment of public and school libraries, and the use of literature in education. The biennial congresses of IBBY have focused on such topics as books and illustrations, books and the school, and children's literature and the developing countries. IBBY serves as an advisor to national and international groups and has consultative relations with UNICEF and Unesco.

The United States Board on Books for Young People is one of over forty national sections of IBBY. It encourages the provision of reading materials of merit to young people throughout the world and cooperates with IBBY and similar organizations. USBBY pays United States dues to IBBY. USBBY was formed in 1984 from two existing groups, the U.S. National Section of IBBY and Friends of IBBY, Inc. The American Library Association (§12) and the Children's Book Council (§35) are charter patron members of USBBY; other members are dues-paying individuals, organizations, businesses, and foundations.

Examples

1) The Hans Christian Andersen Medal for children's authors and illustrators, created by IBBY and awarded annually, is often called the "Little Nobel Prize."

2) The "Books for Language-Retarded Children" collection has been exhibited by IBBY worldwide. This project has been cosponsored with Unesco.

3) IBBY held its 21st World Congress in Oslo in 1988 with the theme "Children's Literature and the New Media."

4) USBBY is planning the 1990 World Congress on Children's Books that will take place in Williamsburg, Virginia, on September 7-9, 1990. The congress will focus on the theme "Literacy through Literature: Children's Books Make a Difference."

Publications

IBBY's publication of record, *Bookbird,* published quarterly; a semiannual newsletter from USBBY; the biennial IBBY Honour List; *The International Directory of Children's Literature Specialists,* issued in 1986; directories; proceedings; and catalogs.

Sources of Support

For both IBBY and USBBY, membership fees and contributions.

---

§54 International Book Committee (IBC)

c/o International Reading Association
701 Dallam Road
Newark, Delaware 19711
Ralph Staiger, *Chairman*
Founded in 1972

What/For Whom

The International Book Committee is an advisory committee of nongovernmental organizations with consultative status to Unesco which are concerned with books and reading. Representatives of international organizations from throughout the book field—for example, the International Federation of Library Associations and Institutions (§55), International PEN (see §80), and the International Reading Association (§57)— are among IBC's sixteen member organizations. IBC was formed as an outgrowth of the 1972 International Book Year support committee and was fundamental in the formulation of the declaration "Towards a Reading Society," adopted by the 1982 World Congress on Books. Reorganized in 1984, IBC is currently aimed at fostering the creating of a reading environment in all types and at all levels of society, one of the targets set by the 1982 world congress. IBC consults with Unesco on book matters and makes recommendations to governments and nongovernmental organizations. IBC awards the International Book Award for outstanding services rendered to the cause of books.

Example	The most recent International Book Award (1988) went to Dina Malhorta, a publisher in India.
Sources of Support	Member organizations may sponsor delegates to meetings of the IBC.

---

§55 International Federation of Library Associations and Institutions (IFLA)

P. O. Box 95312
2509 CH The Hague,
Netherlands
31(70)140884
Paul Nauta, Secretary General
Founded in 1927

What/For Whom

IFLA promotes international cooperation, research, and development in all fields of library activity including bibliography and information services. The multilevel membership includes national library associations and other library institutions, such as libraries, library schools, and bibliographic institutes. IFLA's current activities are in the areas of universal bibliographic control, universal availability of publications, preservation and conservation, and universal data flow and telecommunications. IFLA also devotes concentrated attention to Third World librarians in IFLA, sponsoring projects like an investigation of how to catalog African author's names and preparing curricula for training librarians in developing countries. IFLA has granted consultative status to a number of international organizations concerned with documentation and librarianship.

Examples

1) The Universal Bibliographic Control MARC program promulgates international bibliographic standards, encourages the production of national bibliographies, and aims at standardizing the computerized cataloging of books and other materials. UBC's *International Cataloguing* is published quarterly.

2) The Universal Availability of Publications program facilitates international access to hard-to-obtain publications. It promotes national and international lending programs. The *UAP Newsletter* is published twice a year.

3) The Round Table on Research in Reading, established in 1986, is involved in three major projects: compilation of an international directory of research units engaged in studies on book and library use; young people's reading in transition from childhood to adulthood; and the image of the library.

4) The Children's Libraries Section sponsors Unesco's Books for All program to make the most effective use of available funds by supplying children's books to developing countries.

Publications

IFLA Journal, a quarterly, *IFLA Annual, IFLA Directory* and *IFLA Trends,* (each published every two years), and other serial and monographic publications.

Sources of Support

Funding from Unesco, the Council on Library Resources (§43), and national libraries and membership fees.

§56 International Publishers Association (IPA)

3 Avenue de Miremont
CH-1206 Geneva
Switzerland
022-463018
J. Alexis Koutchoumow, *Secretary-General*
Established in 1896

What/For Whom

The International Publishers Association is a nongovernmental, international organization of national publishing organizations whose objectives are to uphold and defend the freedom of publishers to publish and distribute the works of the mind; to secure international cooperation among members; and to work to overcome illiteracy and the lack of books and shortage of educational materials. It holds a congress every four years to discuss current issues affecting the international book trade, publishing, copyright, and related matters.

Example

The twenty-third IPC Congress, held in London in 1988, drew over six hundred delegates. The principal discussion topics were copyright and the question of intellectual property and piracy, and the need to find a way to satisfy the demand for books. The twenty-fourth congress will be held in New Delhi in 1992.

Publications

International Publishers Bulletin, a quarterly; reports and congress proceedings; monographs such as *Freedom to Publish (La Liberte de Publication)* by Peter Calvocoressi and *Roadmap for the Electronic Publisher* by J. Kist; and *Rights: Copyright and Related Rights,* a quarterly published in cooperation with the International Group of Scientific, Technical, and Medical Publishers (STM).

Source of Support

Membership dues.

§57 International Reading Association (IRA)

800 Barksdale Road, P. O. Box 8139
Newark, Delaware 19714-8139
302-731-1600
Ronald Mitchell, *Executive Director*
Established in 1956

What/For Whom

The International Reading Association is a nonprofit, professional organization which encourages the study of the reading process, research, and better teacher education; promotes the development of reading proficiency to the limit of each person's ability; and works to develop an awareness of the need and importance of reading as a lifetime habit. Its membership of over fifty thousand includes classroom teachers, reading specialists, administrators, educators of reading teachers, reading researchers, parents, librarians, psychologists, and others interested in improving reading instruction. Voluntary committees of IRA explore such subjects as computer technology and reading, early childhood and literacy development, intellectual freedom, parents and reading, reading and literacy, the impact of court decisions on reading, and adult literacy.

Examples

1) The International Reading Association is a member of the Coalition for Literacy (§39).

2) International Reading Association Literacy Award. IRA regularly honors outstanding achievement in fields relating to reading and reading education. Among them is the IRA Literacy Award, presented by Unesco on International Literacy Day each year for outstanding work in the promotion of literacy.

3) Celebrate Literacy. This second IRA literacy award program takes place at the local level. Participating local councils identify and, through an awards ceremony, recognize a local individual, agency, or institution for significant contributions to literacy.

4) IRA also makes other awards for teaching, service to the profession, research, media coverage of reading, and children's book writing. Among them are the Broadcast Media Awards for Radio and Television, which recognize outstanding reporting and programming on radio, television, and cable television that deals with reading and literacy.

5) Reading and the Aging. This Special Interest Group affiliated with the IRA holds meetings at the IRA annual conference and solicits articles, which it publishes in its newsletter. For further information, contact Claire V. Sibold, Editor, 300 Corral de Tierra Road, Salinas, California 93908.

6) National Newspaper in Education Week, cosponsored annually by the IRA and the American Newspaper Publishers Association Foundation (§13), focuses on using newspapers to teach young people to read.

7) IRA was instrumental in setting up a Voluntary Service Committee on Literacy in Third World Countries.

8) The Alpha Upsilon Alpha Honor Society of IRA is sponoring the "From Reader to Reader" project with the Center for the Book in the Library of Congress (§32) in conjunction with the Year of the Young Reader campaign. The goal is to stimulate reading among elementary school children in several states by encouraging them to recommend books to each other via postcard.

9) IRA served as advisor for the Jell-O Desserts Reading Rocket program.

Publications

IRA's four professional journals are *The Reading Teacher,* for elementary school educators, *Journal of Reading,* for those concerned with the teaching of reading at secondary, college, and adult levels, *Reading Research Quarterly,* a technical journal for those interested in reading research; and *Lectura y Vida* ("Reading and Life"), published quarterly in Spanish by the Latin American office in Buenos Aires, Argentina. The bimonthly newspaper *Reading Today* contains news and features about the reading profession. Other publications include reports, bibliographies, critical collections, and other aids for the teacher, some in Spanish. A report *Adult Literacy Education in the United States* was published in 1987.

Sources of Support

Membership dues and fees for publications, advertising, and activities. Funds from private and governmental agencies support only special projects.

---

§58   KIDSNET

6856 Eastern Avenue, N.W., Suite 208
Washington, D.C. 20012
202-291-1400
Karen W. Jaffe, *Executive Director*
Founded in 1984

What/For Whom

KIDSNET is a computerized clearinghouse of information about radio and television programs for children from preschool through high school. Created in cooperation with the National Education Association, KIDSNET has an active database of detailed information on over five thousand programs and public service announcements currently on public, commercial, cable, and syndicated radio and television stations. It also lists programs including documentaries, specials, and mini series that are either relevant to children and youth or appropriate for them.

The archive database offers complete information on over fifteen thousand programs that have previously aired on public or commercial stations and are available for use by educational nonprofit institutions such as schools, libraries, museums, and hospitals. KIDSNET also includes the only complete listing of home video programs targeted to this age group.

KIDSNET is available for access by specialists in children's media, teachers, librarians, media specialists, state and local education administrators, hospitals, museums, parents, and leaders in education, health, social services, and arts communities.

Examples

1) Subscribers can search KIDSNET by subject or curriculum area, target age, and special needs, such as bilingual materials, captioned in another language, or those for the hearing impaired. Listings include literary references to books, plays, and short stories; availability of print materials, such as scripts and bibliographies; program formats, writers; and copyright requirements.

2) KIDSNET offers a Bulletin Board of projects and programs in development or in production for acquisition or instant monitoring of current and future competition in broadcast, cable, and home video markets.

Publications

A quarterly newsletter, users manual, and catalog.

Sources of Support

Grants from foundations and corporations and subscription fees for access to online services.

---

§59 Laubach Literacy Action (LLA)

1320 Jamesville Avenue
Syracuse, New York 13210
315-422-9121
Peter A. Waite, *Executive Director*
Established in 1955

What/For Whom

One of the nation's largest volunteer organizations, Laubach Literacy Action is the United States arm of Laubach Literacy International. LLA combats adult and adolescent illiteracy nationwide by providing basic literacy instruction and English instruction for speakers of other languages, training tutors, publishing educational materials for students and tutors, providing referral services, and disseminating information on literacy. Its network of over fifty thousand volunteers provides tutoring to adult illiterates in forty-six states. Laubach uses its own textbooks and one-on-one method of literacy instruction. Nonreaders and low-reading-level adults not reached by other programs are special concerns of LLA. In addition to promoting adult literacy nationally, LLA has programs that work with community agencies, including public adult education agencies, social service organizations, churches, service clubs, libraries, and prisons. Volunteers are trained both to tutor and to administer programs.

Examples

1) Laubach is a member of the Coalition of Literacy (§39).

2) Laubach expanded on the 1987 Year of the Reader theme initiated by the Center for the Book at the Library of Congress (§32) and declared 1987 the Year of the New Reader to focus on new readers and the challenge literacy students face.

3) The first National Adult Literacy Congress, held September 1987 in Philadelphia, was cosponsored by Laubach, the Center for Literacy, the Mayor's Commission on Literacy in Philadelphia, and Women of the Evangelical Lutheran Church in America (§99). At the congress, a public proclamation was formulated which addressed the problem of adult illiteracy in the United States.

4) LLA has been working with Literacy Volunteers of America (§61) and the federal agency ACTION (§1) to develop administrative training for volunteer leaders of local literacy projects. In cooperation with ACTION and Dayton Hudson Foundation, LLA produced a fourteen-minute video entitled "Making a Difference," developed to recruit and orient retired people to volunteer in adult literacy programs through their local Retired Senior Volunteer Program (RSVP) (see §1).

Publications

New Readers Press, Laubach Literacy International's United States publishing division, produces teaching and tutor-training materials aimed at "new readers" in community-based literacy programs. The press also publishes a weekly newspaper, *News for You,* a quarterly newspaper *Literacy Advance,* a national newsletter, *Students Speaking Out,* for and by literacy students and leisure books written for adults and older youth whose reading skills are at sixth-grade level or lower.

Sources of Support

Individual contributions; membership dues; publications income and donations from corporations and foundations.

§60   Library of Congress

Washington, D.C. 20540
202-707-5000
Established in 1800

What/For Whom

The Library of Congress, the world's largest library, contains more than twenty million books and millions of maps, manuscripts, periodicals, films, recordings, prints, and photographs. It has nearly five thousand employees. Although benefiting from deposits to the Copyright Office of the United States, which is one of its departments, the Library of Congress does not contain a copy of every book printed in the United States. Nevertheless, by the end of its 1987 fiscal year, the Library's collections numbered over eighty-four million items. It is an international library, for it maintains acquisitions offices outside the United States, catalogs books in over 450 languages, and exchanges publications with institutions around the world. It is estimated that two-thirds of the publications currently received by the Library of Congress are in languages other than English.

The Library of Congress is part of the legislative branch of the government. It is both the legislative library for the Congress and "the nation's library," serving readers and researchers not only in Washington but throughout the United States. Library of Congress offices with specialized interests in the creation, preservation, and use of books and in stimulating public interest in books and reading include the American Folklife Center, the Copyright Office, the Preservation Office, the Cataloging-in-Publication Division, the Research Services Department, the National Library Service for the Blind and Physically Handicapped, the Poetry Office, the Publishing Office, the Children's Literature Center (§36), and the Center for the Book (§32).

Examples

1) In 1987, the Copyright Office held public hearings on library photocopying and on the copyrightability of various forms of new technologies.

2) In preservation, the Library's mass deacidification project, a partial solution to the severe problem of deteriorating book paper, continues to receive top priority. *Slow Fires: On the Preservation of the Human Record,* a film sponsored by the Council on Library Resources (§43), the Library of Congress, and the National Endowment for the Humanities (§75), was completed in 1987.

3) After years of research, development, and consumer testing, in 1987 the National Library Service for the Blind and Physically Handicapped began producing a new "easy cassette," machine for readers who have difficulty operating regular cassette players.

80

4) In 1988 Howard Nemerov was named by the Librarian of Congress as the third poet laureate consultant in poetry. Mr. Nemerov's predecessors in this post, established in 1985, are Robert Penn Warren and Richard Wilbur.

5) In carrying out its mission to provide prepublication cataloging information for those titles most likely to be acquired by U.S. libraries, the Cataloging-in-Publication Division reached an all-time high in its coverage of the U.S. book publishing output. In 1987 an estimated 82 percent of the total titles published in the United States were given Cataloging-in-Publication data and five hundred new publishers joined the program.

6) The Publishing Office brought out more than thirty new publications in 1987, including a popular edition of the U.S. Constitution and *The Tradition of Science* by Leonard Bruno, a major study of landmark scientific works in the Library of Congress collections.

Publications

Library of Congress Publications in Print 1987, available without charge from the Library's Central Services Division, lists over six hundred books, pamphlets, and serial titles, sixty-three folk and music recordings, thirty-one literary recordings, and four video recordings.

Sources of Support

Federal government supplemented by gift and trust funds.

---

§61 Literacy Volunteers of America (LVA)

5795 Widewaters Parkway
Syracuse, New York 13214
315-445-8000
Jinx Crouch, *President*
Founded in 1962

What/For Whom

LVA's national organization combats adult illiteracy through a network of local affiliates that offer training and support for community volunteer literacy programs. LVA has over two hundred chapters in thirty-one states. More than thirty thousand tutors and students are involved in its programs. One-on-one instruction is offered in both basic literacy and English as a second language. Literacy Volunteers of America recommends no single method or series of textbooks. The major emphasis in publication is on the development of training materials for program administrators, trainers, and tutors. LVA also provides technical assistance to beginning programs, disseminates literacy information, and provides referral services to potential tutors and students.

Examples

1) LVA is a member of the Coalition for Literacy (§39).

2) Wally Amos, LVA's national spokesman, who is known for his "literacy awareness events," donated 5 percent of the royalties from his autobiography, *The Face That Launched a Thousand Chips,* and 10 percent of the profits from his second book, *Wally Amos's The Power in You* to support the work of LVA.

3) LVA was awarded a Partners in Literacy for Workers with Disabilities grant by the U.S. Department of Labor. This grant allows LVA in cooperation with the Goodwill Industries of America, Inc., to continue programs in which clients of sheltered workshops are learning to read, are upgraded in their work at Goodwill, and are qualifying for work outside the sheltered workshop.

4) Philip Morris Company named LVA as its national charity for the 1988 Virginia Slims tennis tournament series.

5) Video adaptations of the Basic Reading Tutor Training Workshop, financed by public and private funds, enable LVA to train more tutors in remote areas.

6) In conjunction with the Gannett Foundation, LVA created a curriculum and training guide for using newspapers to teach reading.

Publications

LVA publishes the newsletter *The Reader,* several reading series, training manuals, handbooks, and reports.

Sources of Support

Sale of training and support materials; membership fees; fees for technical assistance to nonmember organizations; trust funds; government agency funding for projects; and contributions from foundations, corporations, and individuals.

---

§62 Literary Landmarks Association (LLA)

The Thurber House
77 Jefferson Avenue
Columbus, Ohio 43215
614-228-7458
Donn F. Vickers, *Executive Director*
Established in 1986

What/For Whom

Literary Landmarks Association was founded to help preserve our literary heritage and to promote the literary arts. LLA assists individuals and organizations in local communities to obtain, restore, and promote historic literary sites and to aid in the development of literary programming appropriate to those sites. Major program areas are research, publications, technical assistance for those working on local sites, and literary tours for the general public.

Examples

1) LLA with Friends of Libraries U.S.A. (FOLUSA) (§47) co-sponsored "Texas: A Literary Portrait," a literary reading and reception held during the 1988 midwinter meeting of the American Library Association (§12) in San Antonio. During the 1988 annual conference in New Orleans, LLA and FOLUSA cosponsored a literary walking tour of the French Quarter. Following the tour, the residence of Tennessee Williams was dedicated as a literary landmark.

2) With the Florida Center for the Book, in 1987 the LLA sponsored the dedication of Slip F-18, Bahia Mar, Fort Lauderdale, Florida, as a literary landmark. Slip F-18 was the home of the *Busted Flush,* the houseboat of Travis McGee, the popular fictional hero of Florida author John D. MacDonald.

Publication

Cornerstone, a "seasonal" newsletter, provides profiles of established literary landmarks, book reviews, essays and reports on restoration, and programming activities across the country.

Sources of Support

Membership dues and contributions from individuals.

---

§63 Minnesota Center for Book Arts (MCBA)

24 North Third Street
Minneapolis, Minnesota 55401
612-338-3634
Jim Sitter, *Executive Director*
Founded in 1985

What/For Whom

The Minnesota Center for Book Arts preserves and promotes the book arts, concentrating on hand arts, and educates the public about their aesthetic, social, historic, and commercial aspects. MCBA is a working museum of letterpress printing, hand bookbinding, and hand papermaking. Its workshops are open for tours and classes and available for rental by craftsmen. MCBA also organizes exhibitions and lectures and cooperates with other local institutions that are concerned with graphic arts, rare books, and the history of the book. The Jerome/MCBA fellowship program provides funds for the creation of new book art by writers, visual artists, and book artists at an emerging stage in their career.

Examples	1) MCBA offers classes in papermaking, printing, and binding.
	2) MCBA opened a museum shop in 1986 which features letterpress books, books on the history of printing and on bookmaking processes, handmade papers, and marbled and paste papers.
Publication	*MCBA*, its newsletter, includes announcements of exhibits and classes, the MCBA calendar, and membership information.
Sources of Support	Gifts from local and national corporations and foundations and from individuals; membership fees.

---

§64   Modern Language Association of America (MLA)

10 Astor Place
New York, New York 10003
212-475-9500
Pamela Franklin, *Executive Director*
Established in 1883

What/For Whom

The largest organization of academic professionals in the United States, the MLA is devoted to the study and teaching of literature, languages, and linguistics. Its members are teachers, graduate students, journalists, librarians, administrators, poets, novelists, editors, translators, and other interested professionals, including independent scholars. The MLA provides leadership to the profession in curriculum, teaching, and faculty development through conferences and workshops in its English and foreign-language programs. It educates its members in the development and uses of new technology through publications and programs. It advocates the study of language and literature and the cause of the humanities to Congress, federal agencies, state and local governments, and the media.

MLA divisions encompass various time periods of English, American, and foreign-language literatures and varying approaches for studying them. Among them are: Language and Society; Philosophical Approaches to Literature, including History of Ideas; and Children's Literature. Discussion groups are designed to accommodate the scholarly and professional interests of smaller constituencies within the organization. They focus, for example, on autobiography, biography, and lexicography.

Examples	1) MLA Committee on Academic Freedom. The committee takes action on censorship and freedom of expression issues both within and outside of academe through public statements and the filing of amicus curiae briefs. For example, the committee opposes restrictions on books and instructional approaches and speaks out against threats to teachers' freedom of speech and employment.
	2) In 1988, MLA sponsored a conference "The Right to Literacy" with support from Ohio State University and the Federation of State Humanities Councils (§45). The conference brought together teachers from all levels, researchers, and representatives from state humanities councils, labor unions, and prison literacy programs to address the political, educational, and theoretical issues connected with literacy.
Publications	The quarterly *MLA Newsletter* supplies information about the association and the profession. The journal *PMLA*, published six times a year, contains articles on scholarship and teaching. *Profession,* an annual anthology, publishes articles on professional and pedagogical topics. The *ADE* (Association of Department of English) *Bulletin* and the *ADFL* (Association of Departments of Foreign Languages) *Bulletin* publish articles on professional, pedagogical, curricular, and departmental issues of concern to the profession as a whole. The MLA prepares and publishes many other publications.
Sources of Support	Membership dues, sale of publications, proceeds from conferences, Career Information Service fees; and sale of computer services.

---

§65   National Association for the Preservation and Perpetuation of Storytelling (NAPPS)

P.O. Box 309
Jonesborough, Tennessee 37659
615-753-2171
Jimmy Neil Smith, *Executive Director*
Founded in 1975

What/For Whom	The National Association for the Preservation and Perpetuation of Storytelling is a nonprofit membership organization dedicated to encouraging a greater appreciation, understanding, and practice of storytelling. NAPPS serves as a resource for those individuals and organizations wanting to know more about the art of storytelling, its meaning and importance and

its uses and applications in contemporary America as both an entertainment and an educational tool. The association sponsors a National Storytelling Festival every October, a National Congress on Storytelling in June, and a National Storytelling Institute.

Examples

1) NAPPS seeks to preserve the storytelling tradition through the National Storytelling Resource Center in Jonesborough, Tennessee, which houses archives of storytelling and video and audio tapes and serves as an information center for tellers and those interested in the preservation of folkloric history and its perpetuation as a major art form.

2) The second annual national congress on storytelling in 1988 focused on cultural diversity by examining more closely challenges facing storytellers, organizers, and promoters, such as knowing and understanding the cultural context, meaning, and appropriate setting for stories told outside one's own culture.

Publications

The Yarnspinner, a monthly newsletter with timely information about people, places, and events in storytelling throughout America and the world; *The National Storytelling Journal,* a quarterly focusing on the history, uses, and applications of storytelling; *National Catalog of Storytelling,* a selection of storytelling resources; and the *National Directory of Storytelling,* a resource handbook.

Source of Support

Membership dues.

---

§66   National Association of College Stores (NACS)

528 East Lorain Street
Oberlin, Ohio 44074
216-775-7777
Garis F. Distelhorst, *Executive Director*
Established in 1923

What/For Whom

NACS is a trade association of retail stores that sell books, supplies, and other merchandise to students and faculties of educational institutions. Members also include publishers and suppliers to the college store market. The association was established to educate and aid college stores in achieving professional, profitable operation; to encourage open involvement and cooperation with college administration, faculty, students, and the community at large; and to promote greater awareness of the educational and financial contributions to their schools made by college stores. Though the association is nonprofit, it manages NACSCORP, a member-service, for-profit subsidiary that distributes books, computer software, calendars, and student-rate magazine subscription cards. NACS also conducts professional management seminars throughout the year for college store managers and sponsors an annual conference.

Examples

1) NACS promotes reading to the college market by encouraging member stores to do book promotions in conjunction with the American Library Association's Banned Books campaign (see §12). NACS also contributes to Reading Is Fundamental (§85), which focuses on children from the age of three through the high school years.

2) The first NACS General Booksellers Conference was held May 1988 during the annual conference of the American Booksellers Association (§7). Forums focused on practical suggestions on general bookselling in college stores.

3) NACS launched a major promotion contest for the 1985 television program "Robert Kennedy and His Times" in cooperation with the CBS Television/Library of Congress "Read More About It" book project, administered by the Center for the Book in the Library of Congress (§32). The winning store manager received a trip to Washington, D.C.

Publications

The College Store Journal is a trade magazine issued six times a year. The *College Store Buyers' Guide, Book Buyers' Manual,* and *NACS Weekly Bulletin* keep members informed of developments and activities in the industry and the association and among members. Featured regularly in the *Bulletin* is an account of what books are being read on campus, based upon a tabulation compiled by *The Chronicle of Higher Education,* with comparable positions shown for *The New York Times* and *Publishers Weekly* listings. *The Campus Market Report* is a monthly newsletter for campus watchers and the NACS *Campus Focus* provides information pertinent to college and library administrators.

Sources of Support

Membership dues, seminar fees, sale of publications, and NACSCORP operations.

§67

National Book Awards, Inc. (NBA)

155 Bank Street
Studio 1002d
New York, New York 10014
212-206-0024
Barbara Prete, *Executive Director*

What/For Whom

National Book Awards, Inc., is a nonprofit, charitable organization that encourages reading and participation in the literary arts through making writers and books newsworthy and exciting to the general public. First established in 1955 and known as both the National (1955-80) and then the American Book Awards (1981-86), the organization returned to its original name of National Book Awards on January 1, 1987, when it became a not-for-profit institution. The NBA strives to bring books to the forefront of American consciousness. The NBA sponsors two major projects: the Literary Awards and the Media Program. The annual awards program honors books by bestowing a ten-thousand-dollar prize upon American writers in two categories: fiction and nonfiction. The Literary Media program is designed to further increase the general level of interest in reading and to activate wider public participation in the literary arts.

Examples

1) The Literary Media program's pilot project of public service advertisements, in print and on television, led to the development of a syndicated weekly radio show that features book authors and their ideas and philosophies. A literary exhibit, entitled "Voices of American Writers" and sponsored with the American Library Association (§12), reflects on the writer within American society over the last four decades.

2) NBA has reestablished National Book Week, which will be celebrated each year the week following Thanksgiving.

3) During National Book Week in 1988, the NBA and the Center for the Book in the Library of Congress (§32) sponsored the first annual National Book Week lecture. Held at the Library of Congress the evening before the 1989 National Book Awards were presented in New York City, the lecture had as its first speaker Richard Rhodes, 1988 winner of the National Book Award.

Sources of Support

Financial assistance from American corporations and individuals.

§68 National Book Critics Circle (NBCC)

756 South Tenth Street
Philadelphia, Pennsylvania 19147
215-925-8406
Alida Becker, *Vice President/Secretary*
Founded in 1974

What/For Whom

The National Book Critics Circle is a national professional not-for-profit association of book critics and book review editors. NBCC has about five hundred members. It aims at elevating standards of book reviewing, promoting public awareness of good book criticism, and improving communication between publishers and reviewers.

Examples

1) The annual presentation of awards in biography, criticism, fiction, nonfiction, and poetry is the best known NBCC program.

2) In 1987, NBCC conducted a survey of its membership on basic issues of ethics in book reviewing.

3) In 1985, NBCC launched a campaign to encourage publishers to name reviewers, not just newspapers, when quoting reviews for jacket, flap, or advertising copy and to encourage publishers to be more scrupulous in excerpting quotations for such copy.

Publication

A quarterly journal.

Source of Support

Membership fees.

§69 National Coalition Against Censorship (NCAC)

132 West Forty-third Street
New York, New York 10036
212-944-9899
Leanne Katz, *Executive Director*
Established in 1974

What/For Whom

NCAC is an alliance of national organizations, including religious, educational, professional, artistic, labor, and civil rights groups, committed to defending freedom of thought, inquiry, and expression. The coalition educates its own members about the dangers of censorship and how to oppose them and uses the mass media to inform the general public about censorship issues. Other coalition activities include conferences, program assistance, advocacy, and the monitoring of legislation with First Amendment implications at both national and state levels. NCAC compiles and disseminates educational material, including information packets on many First Amendment-related issues, among them creationism, women and pornography, guidelines for selecting educational materials, government secrecy, and censorship and black literature.

Example   NCAC's Clearinghouse on School Book-Banning Litigation collects and makes available to librarians, journalists, lawyers, educators, school boards, parents, and the public at large up-to-date information on the status of school censorship cases and appropriate legal documents.

Publications   The quarterly newsletter *Censorship News;* periodic reports and background papers; and *Books on Trial: A Survey of Recent Cases,* a source of information on litigation arising from censorship in private schools in the United States, with a listing of books, magazines, and films involved. *Books on Trial* complements NCAC's earlier publication, *Report on Book Censorship Litigation in Public Schools.*

Sources of Support   Individual contributions, sale of publications, conference fees, and grants.

---

§70 National Commission on Libraries and Information Science (NCLIS)

1111 Eighteenth Street, N.W., Suite 310
Washington, D.C. 20036
202-254-3100
Susan Martin, *Executive Director*
Established in 1970

What/For Whom   NCLIS is a permanent, independent agency of the United States government, established by Public Law 91-345 to advise the President and Congress on library and information policies and plans in order to meet the needs of all United States citizens. In its second decade, NCLIS program objectives center on the library and information needs of special constituencies, such as cultural minorities, the elderly, and rural Americans. The commission believes that its goal of equal access to library and information services for all citizens implies universal literacy and therefore works with members of the library and information community and various agencies of the executive branch on literacy programs. Another focus of NCLIS is the new technologies and their applications to the library and information field.

Examples

1) Activities with ACTION (§1). NCLIS and ACTION have agreed to work cooperatively at the national level through their respective networks to promote the improvement and better use of library and information services to the elderly through voluntary activities. Similar agreements, signed in 1985 with the Administration on Aging and the U.S. Department of Health and Human Services, resulted in improved cooperation between libraries and agencies that serve the aging at the state and local levels. In late 1988, NCLIS and ACTION joined to create the "RSVP Intergenerational Library Assistance Project" to help libraries in several U.S. cities provide assistance to children who use libraries after school. Individual libraries work with the Retired Seniors Volunteer Program (see §1) to identify needs of local children and develop plans to use volunteers in literacy development, drug education, homework assistance, and other areas.

2) National Rural Information Services Development Program. The focus of this program is on improving the delivery of library and information services to rural citizens. Under this program, the rural library takes on the role of a comprehensive community learning/information center that uses the latest computer and telecommunications technologies. Functioning as a catalyst in this cooperative program, NCLIS works closely with the library and information community, the U.S. Department of Agriculture, the cooperative extension services, and the nations's state universities and land-grant colleges.

3) Literacy activity. The commission advises the U. S. Department of Education (§95) in its coordination of the Adult Literacy Initiative (see §95), is a member of the Coalition for Literacy (§39), and is a sponsor of Project Literacy U.S. (PLUS) (§83). Another effort to promote literacy, the U.S. Army/NCLIS Reading Project was coordinated with the Department of Defense and used federally developed computer technology in both an urban and a rural public library setting to assist in tutoring adults and out-of-school teens whose basic reading skills were between zero and fifth grade level.

4) NCLIS is a cosponsor with the American Library Association (§12) of the National Library Card Sign-Up campaign.

5) NCLIS and the Center for the Book in the Library of Congress (§32) cosponsored the publication of George Nash's *Books and the Founding Fathers,* a lecture presented on November 1, 1987, to mark the Year of the Reader and the Bicentennial of the U.S. Constitution. Nash, the official biographer of Herbert Hoover, was appointed in 1987 as a commissioner of NCLIS.

Publications

Reports, articles, and special publications.

Source of support

Federal government.

§71 National Council for Families and Television (NCFT)

Suite 300
3801 Barham Boulevard
Los Angeles, California 90068
213-876-5959
Tricia Robin, *President*
Established in 1977

What/For Whom

The National Council for Families and Television is a non-profit, nonadversarial educational organization whose goal is to enhance the quality of family life in the United States by positively affecting the creation and uses of primetime entertainment television. NCFT brings together television's creative community and other groups with an important interest in family life. In support of its mission, NCFT sponsors a Listeners Bureau, acts as a referral service, cohosts symposia, and hosts an annual conference.

Example

The 1987 conference focused on "Television, Families and Work" and was attended by programming creators, broadcasters, business leaders, educators, social scientists, and others with an important interest in family life.

Publications

Television & Families, a quarterly, is a forum for information, research, and opinion. *NCFT Information Service Bulletin,* a monthly intended as an educational tool, includes news, features, research abstracts, and reprinted articles aimed at television writers, story developers, producers, and programming executives.

Sources of Support

Contributions from individuals, corporations, and foundations.

§72 National Council of Teachers of English (NCTE)

1111 Kenyon Road
Urbana, Illinois 61801
217-328-3870
L. Jane Christensen, *Associate Executive Director*
Established in 1911

What/For Whom

NCTE is a nonprofit professional service organization committed to improving the teaching of literature and the English language. It emphasizes the need to teach English as both a system of language skills and a humane discipline. Most of NCTE's one hundred thousand members are English teachers, teacher educators, and researchers.

The NCTE provides information on the teaching of English and sponsors conferences and two major conventions annually. Committees and task forces conduct and encourage research on topics including composition, media, and reading. Liaison committees carry out projects with other professional groups such as the International Reading Association (§57).

Examples

1) NCTE has collaborated with the International Reading Association on a statement warning against the use of unreliable readability formulas for textbooks to determine what children can and should read.

2) NCTE sponsors achievement awards for excellence in writing, student literary magazines, and research in the teaching of English.

Publications

Eight monthly or quarterly professional journals, pamphlets, books, newsletters, and cassettes. Among the journals are *College English,* a monthly aimed at the college scholar and teacher; *English Journal,* a monthly presenting the latest developments in teaching reading at the middle, junior high, and senior high school levels; *Language Arts,* monthly, for elementary school reading and language teachers and teacher trainers; *SLATE Newsletter,* six times a year, summarizing national news affecting English language arts educators; and *Quarterly Review of Double Speak,* which includes articles, book reviews, and other materials dealing with double speak.

Sources of Support

Membership dues, sale of publications, and conference fees.

---

§73 National Council on the Aging, Inc. (NCOA)

600 Maryland Avenue, S.W., West Wing 100
Washington, D.C. 20024
202-479-1200
Sylvia Liroff, *Manager Older Adult Education*
Established in 1950

What/For Whom

NCOA is a private, nonprofit organization that serves as a major resource for information, training, technical assistance, advocacy, publication, and research on every aspect of aging. Individual members range from senior center professionals, health care practitioners, and other service providers to gerontologists, agency board members, and personnel directors. Organizational members include adult day care centers; senior housing facilities; senior centers; older work employment services; and local, state, and national organizations and companies serving the aging.

Examples

1) Literacy Education for the Elderly Project (LEEP) offers reading instruction to older adults and trains them as tutors. Begun in 1984 and supported by a grant from the Fund for the Improvement of Postsecondary Education (FIPSE), an agency of the U.S. Department of Education, this national program links the resources of community-based organizations already serving large numbers of older people and the local affiliates of national adult literacy organizations (for example, Laubach Literary Action [§59] or Literacy Volunteers of America [§61]). A distinctive feature of the program is that older volunteers serve as reading instructors for the older adults who receive tutoring.

2) Discovery through the Humanities Program is a reading-centered, community discussion program for older adults that focuses on the humanities. The program is intended to expand and diversify the offerings of senior centers, nursing homes, day care centers, nutrition sites, retirement complexes, and other organizations serving older people. Begun in 1976 and known formerly as the Senior Center Humanities Program or SCHP, the program is supported by a grant from the General Programs Division of the National Endowment for the Humanities (§75). Additional funding comes from participating senior centers and sponsoring agencies and from corporations and foundations.

3) Educational Goals Inventory (EGI) is a computer-assisted method for setting educational goals that is used by organizations serving older adults. Senior centers, nursing homes, churches, libraries, and housing centers use the inventory, which was developed by the Educational Testing Service of Princeton, New Jersey, to help them plan and improve educational programs for senior citizens. For example, the inventory could help libraries figure out how to reach older adults in the community; how to work with other community organizations, such as senior citizen centers, in reaching older adults; or how to assess the quality of education programs being offered older adults. The EGI grew out of a two-year project, "Nontraditional Education Programs for the Elderly," supported by FIPSE.

Publications

The bimonthly magazine *Perspective on Aging* examines issues, research, and programs on aging. *Collage: Cultural Enrichment and Older Adults,* a publication of the Discovery through the Humanities Program and the National Center on the Arts and the Aging, is issued three times a year. The quarterly annotated bibliography *Current Literature on Aging* lists the most recent books, articles, and periodicals on gerontology. NCOA has also developed a series of publications to help organize literacy programs especially for older adults.

Sources of Support

Grants from the federal government and from foundations, membership dues, contributions from participating organizations, sale of program guidebooks, software computer programs, and publications, and conferences.

§74 National Endowment for the Arts (NEA)

Nancy Hanks Center
1100 Pennsylvania Avenue, N.W.
Washington, D.C. 20506
202-682-5451
Stephen Goodwin, *Director, Literature Program*
Established in 1965

What/For Whom

NEA is an independent federal agency established to encourage and assist the nation's cultural resources. NEA carries out its mission through grant programs and a wide range of leadership and advocacy activities. It also serves as a national forum to assist in the exchange of ideas and as a catalyst to promote the best developments in the arts and education. NEA's mission is accomplished through fellowships awarded to individuals of exceptional artistic talent and grants awarded to nonprofit cultural organizations representing the highest quality in such fields as design arts, education, dance, folk arts, literature, media arts, museums, music, opera, theater, and the visual arts.

Examples

1) NEA awards fellowships for creative writers in fiction, poetry, and other creative prose.

2) Literary publishing. Assistance to Literary Magazines grants help nonprofit literary magazines that regularly publish poetry, fiction, literary essays, and translations. Small Press Assistance grants support small, independent presses that publish contemporary creative writing. In November 1986, the NEA Literature Program and the Center for the Book in the Library of Congress (§32) cosponsored a seminar on Book Distribution and Literary Publishing.

3) Audience development. One program, Residences for Writers, funds residencies, lasting between one week and one year, for published writers of poetry, fiction, creative essays, and other creative prose. NEA is especially interested in projects that support public readings outside large urban centers and in traditionally underserved communities. Cultural organizations at which residencies are located include state arts agencies, colleges, universities, libraries, museums, art centers, radio and television stations, and other professional and community organizations. The program is designed to develop audiences for contemporary writers both in their own communities and in other parts of the country. Another kind of audience development grant supports such projects as regional small press book fairs, principally outside large urban areas.

4) PEN Syndicated Fiction Project. The project is a cooperative effort of the PEN American Center (§80), a major writer's service organization, and the Literature Program of the NEA.

Judges from PEN select short stories from those submitted in a national competition, and the endowment offers them free to a dozen or so newspapers each month for national syndication to over seven million readers. Authors whose stories are selected receive money from the endowment and additional funds from each newspaper that prints them. For further information contact Caroline Marshall, Director, Syndicated Fiction Project, P.O. Box 6303, Washington, D.C. 20015; 202-543-6322.

Publications

The Arts Review is NEA's quarterly review of developments in the arts and progress on endowment-supported projects. In addition, NEA publishes grant application information, available from specific discipline programs.

Source of Support

Federal government.

---

§75   National Endowment for the Humanities (NEH)

Nancy Hanks Center
1100 Pennsylvania Avenue, N.W.
Washington, D.C. 20506
202-786-0271
Thomas C. Phelps, *Program Officer, Libraries and Archives, Division of General Programs*
Established in 1965

What/For Whom

NEH is an independent federal agency established to promote the humanities through grants to humanities projects and scholars in defined areas of humanistic study. These areas include, but are not limited to, "languages, both modern and classical; linguistics; literature; history; jurisprudence; philosophy; archaeology; comparative religion; ethics; the history, criticism, and theory of the arts; those aspects of the social sciences which have humanistic content and employ humanistic methods; and the study and application of the humanities to the human environment with particular attention to the relevance of the humanities to the current conditions of national life." Grants are made through five divisions: Education Programs, Fellowships and Seminars, General Programs, Research Programs, and State Programs; and two offices: the Office of Challenge Grants and the Office of Preservation.

Examples

1) The Office of Preservation provides national leadership and grant support for the preservation of deteriorating books and other paper documents in libraries, archives, museums, historical organizations, and other repositories.

2) The Division of Fellowships and Seminars supports scholars, teachers, and others undertaking independent research.

3) The Division of General Programs. Its programs include:

a) Humanities Projects in Libraries. These are programs through which all types of libraries serving adults—public, community college, university, and special libraries—enhance their community's appreciation and knowledge of the humanities. Another goal is to increase the appreciation and use of library collections. In 1987, thirty grants were awarded for humanities projects in libraries.

A Humanities Project in Libraries grant in 1987 funded the New England Foundation for the Humanities to support a series of reading and discussion programs in libraries throughout the region focusing on the framing of the U. S. Constitution as revealed through biographies, original documents, historical writings, and other literature.

b) Humanities Projects in Media. Projects involve the planning, scripting, or production of television, radio, or film programs in the humanities intended for national distribution and general audiences. Of special interest are programming for children and programs that dramatize or examine classic works of fiction and nonfiction for television and radio.

4) The Division of Research Programs has programs of interest as well.

a) Reference Materials. The program funds the preparation of reference works that will result in the advancement of research and learning in the humanities among professionals and the general public.

b) Subsidies to scholarly publishers. NEH gives grants to university and private presses for publication of books on humanities topics that they would not otherwise be able to publish.

5) Division of State Programs. The division supports humanities programs in individual states. Grants are awarded through a network of humanities councils.

Publications

The magazine *Humanities* is the endowment's bimonthly review of current work and thought in the humanities. It also describes recent grants and progress on projects supported by endowment funding. In addition, NEH publishes grant application information and a variety of special publications.

Source of Support

Federal government.

§76

National Information Standards Organization/Z39 (NISO)

National Bureau of Standards
Administration 101, Library E-106
Gaithersburg, Maryland 20899
301-975-2814
Patricia Harris, *Executive Director*
Established in 1939

What/For Whom

The National Information Standards Organization/Z39 is a nonprofit association which develops technical standards used in a wide range of information services and products. The standards address the communication needs of libraries, information services, publishing, and the book trade in such areas as: information transfer, forms and records, identification systems, publication formats, transliteration, preservation of materials, and library equipment and supplies. NISO's sixty members include libraries; professional, technical, and educational associations; abstracting and indexing services; publishers; government agencies; and commercial and industrial organizations. NISO participates in the International Organization for Standardization (ISO). Over twenty projects are in progress, some which involve the development of entirely new standards and others the revision of older ones. The NISO Archives are located in the University of Maryland Library where they are accessible to qualified researchers and students.

Examples

1) NISO promotes and encourages the use of the infinity symbol inside a circle ∞ as the symbol identifying a publication printed on paper that will last several hundred years and meets the criteria for permanence set forth in the NISO-developed standard Z39.48.

2) The international standard book number, ISBN, and international standard serial number, ISSN, which facilitate the handling of books and periodicals at all levels of distribution, were defined by Z39 standards.

3) NISO is developing a standard for hardcover case bindings in order to describe the binding materials, methods, and structures that will contribute to durability of a publication in a library setting.

Publications

Over forty-five reports of standards are in print. *Information Standards Quarterly* (formerly *Voice of Z39*) provides ongoing information about NISO activities.

Sources of Support

Membership fees and grants from the federal government and foundations.

§77   National PTA

700 North Rush Street
Chicago, Illinois 60611-2571
312-787-0977
Tari Marshall, *Director of Public Relations*
Established in 1897

What/For Whom

The National PTA is a volunteer association that seeks to unite home, school, and community in promoting the education, health, and safety of children. Working through national, state, and local PTA associations, the organization is active in child advocacy causes. These include securing child labor laws; supporting compulsory public education, including kindergarten; creating a national public health service and developing health, safety, and nutrition programs for children; promoting education for children with special needs; providing parenthood education; organizing and improving school libraries; and establishing a juvenile justice system. The association is also concerned with the issues of latchkey children, discipline, and parent and community involvement in education. Most PTA members are parents, but some are teachers, school administrators, students, senior citizens, and individuals with or without children.

Examples

1) The Big City PTA Project was initiated in 1987 to strengthen urban PTAs and reach out to parents who have not been traditionally involved in their children's literature.

2) National PTA presents its Reading Award to a local unit that has conducted an outstanding reading program. The award recognizes PTAs that have trained parents to help their children become readers, that have developed creative ways to increase an interest in reading by students, and that host cooperative projects between schools and libraries.

Publications

The association's magazine, *PTA Today,* published seven times a year; the newsletter *What's Happening in Washington,* which keeps PTA members informed about pending federal legislation affecting children and youth; brochures on evaluating schools, juvenile justice systems, television, preschool development, and other subjects; and other newsletters, reports, brochures, planning kits and guides.

Sources of Support

Membership dues, sale of publications, proceeds from conventions, and foundation assistance.

§78 OPAM America, Inc.

1714 Amwell Road P. O. Box 5657
Somerset, New Jersey 08875-5657
201-873-8080
Rev. John Bertello, *IMC*
OPAM founded in 1972; OPAM America established in 1985

What/For Whom

OPAM America is an affiliate of OPAM, an international organization whose purpose is to combat illiteracy throughout the world and foster basic education. OPAM is an acronym for the original Italian name "Opera di Promozione della Alfabetizzazione nel Mondo," which means Organization for the Promotion of World Literacy. OPAM expands the accepted definition of illiterate person as one who does not know how to read, write, or compute mathematically to include one who is also ignorant of any and all of those aspects of life which contribute to the benefit and development of the person, community, society, and country. OPAM promotes community development especially in developing countries through centers for literacy, schools of agronomy and crafts, professional technical instruction, domestic science and hygiene schools, and centers for women's development. OPAM operates by providing resources—money, tools, books, and so on—to groups already operating in the field, mostly missionaries. Founded by Msgr Carlo Muratore, OPAM provides support not only to Catholic missionaries but to Protestant missionaries and others as well. OPAM America educates Americans about the extent of world illiteracy and its results and raises funds for literacy projects.

Example

Project No. 7 in Eutaw, Alabama, is a series of evening classes in domestic science and gardening for teenagers. The purpose of the project is to improve reading and writing capabilities of the teenagers of this rural area.

Sources of Support

Contributions from individuals, organizations, foundations, and institutions and annual membership pledges.

§79 Paideia Group

Institute for Philosophical Research
101 East Ontario Street
Chicago, Illinois 60611
312-337-4102
John Van Doren, *Senior Fellow, Institute for Philosophical Research*
Established in 1979

What/For Whom

The Paideia Group is an informal group of twenty-two nationally recognized educators committed to a special agenda for improving the United States education system at all levels, kindergarten through grade twelve. The group's 1982 manifesto for educational reform calls for a three-part teaching process in which lectures and textbook assignments are only the first step, to be followed by, second, coaching, to form the habits through which skills are permanently mastered, and, third, Socratic teaching, a seminar format in which students answer questions and discuss the answers. The proposal is aimed at eliminating the inequities of the two-track system of schooling, which educates collegebound students in one way and those who are not intending to enter college in another. Paideia's overall purpose is not only to improve the quality of basic schooling in the United States but also to make that quality accessible to all children, without assumptions about whether they are ultimately "destined for labor" or "destined for leisure and learning."

The Paideia Group is headquartered at the Institute for Philosophical Research, which was founded in 1952 by Mortimer J. Adler to explore key philosophical concepts such as freedom, love, happiness, and progress as they are regarded by the most renowned authors of Western civilization. Mr. Adler, director of the Institute for Philosophical Research and chairman of the Board of Editors of Encyclopedia Britannica, is also chairman of the Paideia Group.

Example

1) The Paideia program has been implemented in two high schools and two elementary schools in Chicago as well as in schools from Oakland, California, to Atlanta, Georgia.

2) The National Center for the Paideia program was established on September 1, 1988, at the University of North Carolina, Chapel Hill. The new center coordinates training, research, and communication of the Paideia program and is planning a nationwide network and forum for people devoted to the Paideia movement.

Publications

The Paideia Bulletin: News and Ideas for the Paideia Network, a bimonthly, the Paideia Trilogy, a series by Mortimer Adler explaining the Paideia agenda for educational reform—*The Paideia Proposal* (1982), *Paideia Problems and Possibilities* (1983), and *The Paideia Program* (1984)]—*Seven Steps toward a Paideia School,* and other publications.

Sources of Support

The Paideia Group is funded through the Institute for Philosophical Research by contributions from corporations, foundations, and individuals.

PEN American Center

568 Broadway
New York, New York 10012
212-334-1660
John Morrone, *Programs and Publications*
Established in 1921

What/For Whom

PEN American Center is the largest of more than eighty centers that make up PEN International, founded in London by John Galsworthy to foster understanding among men and women of letters in all countries. Members of PEN work for freedom of expression wherever it has been endangered. International PEN is the only worldwide organization of writers and the chief voice of the literary community. The membership of PEN American Center includes poets, playwrights, editors, essayists, novelists, translators, and editors and agents who have made a substantial contribution to the literary community. Membership is by invitation. PEN's activities include public literary events, conferences, international congresses, literary awards, and assistance to writers in prison and to American writers in financial need. Among the awards PEN gives are the Ernest Hemingway Foundation Award for first novels and the PEN/Faulkner Award for fiction.

Examples

1) Freedom-to-Write, working on behalf of approximately eighty writers in forty countries each year, is actively engaged in protesting the harassment of writers worldwide with letter and cable campaigns, missions by American authors to foreign countries, press releases and press conferences, public events, case sheets, country reports and monthly bulletins. It fights book-banning in libraries and schools around the United States and offers testimony in Congress on issues affecting writers.

2) The Prison Writing Program administers an annual writing competition for incarcerated writers and provides information and referrals to inmates about writing and publishing.

3) The Children's Book Authors' Committee sponsors regular public events focusing on the art of writing for children and young adults and on the diversity of literature for juvenile readers.

4) PEN Syndicated Fiction Project is cooperative venture of the PEN American Center and the Literature Program of the National Endowment for the Arts (§74) which promotes the reading of fiction of contemporary American writers by syndicating short stories in newspapers around the country. PEN judges select the short stories in national competition, and the endowment distributes them for syndication and also directly compensates the writers.

5) In 1988, the growing PEN west coast chapter was officially named PEN Center U.S.A. West.

Publications

The PEN Newsletter, a quarterly, the *Freedom-to-Write Bulletin,* published irregularly, *Grants and Awards Available to American Writers,* a biennial directory, and many reports, pamphlets, and books.

Sources of Support

Sale of publications and videotapes; contributions from individuals, corporations, and foundations; and, for the PEN Syndicated Fiction Project, funding from National Endowment for the Arts.

---

§81   The Philadelphia Book Clinic

Lea and Febiger
600 Washington Square
Philadelphia, Pennsylvania 19106
215-925-8700
Thomas Colaiezzi, *Secretary-Treasurer*
Founded in 1937

What/For Whom

The Philadelphia Book Clinic is an organization devoted to the analysis and solution of problems in the book industry. The clinic's objective is to improve theories of design, production, and distribution and to keep abreast of the newest materials and techniques used to produce a high quality book at a reasonable cost. Members of the clinic, who represent publishing in the Delaware Valley, are involved in the business of producing books from acquisitions, copy editing, production, sales, and distribution of books to work in the industries devoted to supplying the varied materials and services required in book manufacture.

Example

At monthly meetings during the fall, winter, and spring, speakers are invited to address contemporary issues in publishing. The clinic's season culminates with the annual Philadelphia Book Show, a selection of books by Delaware Valley publishers produced in the previous year which represent the best in their fields.

Publication

Catalog of the annual book show.

Source of Support

Membership dues.

§82   Poets & Writers, Inc.

201 West Fifty-fourth Street
New York, New York 10019-5564
212-757-1766
Elliot Figman, *Director*
Established in 1970

What/For Whom

Poets & Writers, Inc., is a nonprofit service organization for the United States literary community. It publishes materials on practical topics related to writing, such as copyright, literary agents, literary bookstores, workshop sponsors, grants, and taxes. It helps pay writers' fees for public readings and workshops in New York State and provides assistance to groups wishing to start such programs. It supplies addresses, facts, and referrals of interest to the writing community nationwide.

Examples

1) Readings/Workshops Program. With principal support from the Literature Program of the New York State Council on the Arts and additional private contributions, the program pays fees to writers who give readings or workshops sponsored by groups in New York State. The purpose of the program is to develop audiences for contemporary literature and to help writers survive financially.

2) Information Center. The center will supply free of charge, over the telephone, facts or information about the professional side of writers' lives, provide writers' current addresses, and answer questions relating to writers' practical needs.

Publications

Poets & Writers Magazine (formerly *Coda: Poets & Writers Newsletter*), published six times a year, provides practical news and comments on publishing, jobs, grants, taxes, and other topics. The organization also publishes reference books, sourcebooks, and guides.

Sources of Support

Grants from the Literature Program of the National Endowment for the Arts (§74) and the Literature Program of the New York State Council on the Arts and contributions from corporations, foundations, and individuals.

§83 Project Literacy U.S. (PLUS)

4802 Fifth Avenue
Pittsburgh, Pennsylvania 15213
412-622-1492
Margot Woodwell, *PBS Project Director*
John E. Harr, *ABC Project Director*
Established in 1985

What/For Whom

PLUS is a national public service campaign being undertaken jointly by Capital Cities/ABC and the Public Broadcasting Service (PBS) to combine local community efforts with a national media focus on combatting the problem of adult literacy in the United States. PLUS has three goals: to raise national awareness of the problem of adult functional illiteracy in America, to develop and encourage volunteer action to address illiteracy, and to encourage those who need help to participate. Both ABC and PBS provide on-air national coverage of the illiteracy problem in all varieties of news and informational programming as well as public service announcements. PLUS has a membership of 117 national support organizations drawn from broadcasters and literacy service providers and a broad-based coalition of community leaders which form the Public Television Outreach Alliance made up of 360 local task forces.

Examples

1) PLUS is a member of the Coalition for Literacy (§39).

2) In 1988, the third year of PLUS, programming and community activities were titled "Youth/Plus." Attention was focused on key problems facing youth in which illiteracy is a connecting thread, including teen pregnancy, dropping out of school, substance abuse, unemployment, and delinquency.

3) PLUS task forces hosted thousands of local business and labor leaders at PLUS business breakfasts throughout the United States to encourage the business community to join and support local literacy activities. A national PLUS business breakfast was hosted by Mrs. Barbara Bush.

4) PLUS cosponsored "The American Seminar—A National Teleconference: Literacy, Your Community, and Its Workforce," with the American Association of Community and Junior Colleges, the National Association of Private Industry Councils, and other national organizations. The purpose of the teleconference was to bring together literacy leaders in every community.

Publications

PLUS quarterly newsletter and monthly update and a PLUS directory of contact people.

Source of Support

Contributions from corporations.

§84 Push Literacy Action Now (PLAN)

1332 G Street, S.E.
Washington, D.C. 20003
202-547-8903
Michael R. Fox, *Executive Director*
Established in 1972

What/For Whom

PLAN is a nonprofit literacy program for adults that serves the community of the District of Columbia and also addresses literacy problems on a national scale. Primarily a volunteer organization, it provides tutoring, testing, information and referral services, teacher training, and advocacy. Believing that one-on-one literacy teaching is neither successful nor economically efficient, PLAN emphasizes small-group classes. Instruction is provided to individuals in-house and to local companies in the workplace. The focus is on adults reading below the sixth-grade level.

PLAN's program emphasizes the need for changes in the society that surrounds those who cannot read. PLAN advocates acceptance of new regulations governing the readability of printed matter for the general public and teaches workshops in writing and analyzing welfare and school reports, manuals, legal and insurance documents, and other communications for more widespread readability. PLAN also urges that literacy be regarded as a basic rather than a support service. To attract greater numbers of people to literacy instruction, for example, PLAN believes that it will be necessary to provide them with support services such as transportation and child care.

Examples

1) Operation Wordwatch is a program designed to enhance literacy for marginally literate adults by increasing the readability of public information routinely written at or near a college reading level and often in an indirect style.

2) Take Up Reading Now (TURN) is designed to bring attention to the needs of low-literate, low-income parents and their children. This program has three parts: Take PART (Parents As Reading Teachers) includes public awareness activities and special training for low-literate parents of children six months to two years; Take CARE (Child Advocacy for Reading Education) offers support to parents of children in lower grades; and Take a BOOK is a "one-way, take-a-book" library for at-risk children living in low-income neighborhoods.

Publications

PLAN's bimonthly newsletter *The Ladder*, distributed nationally, offers incisive, often controversial reviews of literacy programs and developments. *A Look at Illiteracy in America Today: The*

Problem, the Solutions, the Alternatives, a position paper, takes a critical look at the adult literacy effort in the United States and provides suggestions for change.

Sources of Support

Contributions from foundations, community groups, corporations, and individuals and minimal tuition fees paid by students.

---

§85 Reading Is Fundamental, Inc. (RIF)

Smithsonian Institution
600 Maryland Avenue, S.W., Suite 500
Washington, D.C. 20560
202-287-3220
Ruth Graves, *President*
Anne Richardson, *Chairman of the Board*
Established in 1966

What/For Whom

Founded by Margaret S. McNamara and affiliated with the Smithsonian Institution, RIF is a private, nonprofit, nationwide organization that inspires children to read and to aspire through reading. RIF reaches youngsters by ensuring that they have books in their homes; providing activities to stimulate reading interest; making it possible for children to choose and own books; encouraging reading for pleasure; and involving parents in their children's reading. The national RIF organization has helped start RIF projects in schools, libraries, hospitals, day-care centers, correctional facilities, and migrant farmworker communities. The projects are run largely by volunteers and involve parents, educators, librarians, and business and civic leaders. RIF projects include book distributions, festive occasions when youngsters select and keep books that they like, and reading-related activities at the grassroots level, for example, dramatic skits, poster and essay contests, and talks on reading by athletes and entertainers. RIF offers local projects guidance materials and workshops, special discounts and services from book suppliers, information on reading motivation techniques, and support by a nationwide campaign to promote reading through public service announcements on television and in the print media.

Examples

1) Reading Is Fun Week. This annual nationwide celebration of reading is highlighted by the presentation of the In Celebration of Reading award. The award is presented to the youngster who has exceeded specified reading requirements. The celebration program is designed to encourage youngsters to read, outside of school hours, books unconnected with school assignments.

2) RIF benefited in a partnership formed between American Express and Waldenbooks. The two companies each donated to RIF five cents on every purchase at a Waldenbooks store made with an American Express card.

3) RIF served as consultant for the Jell-O Desserts Family Reading Survey, a nationwide poll conducted by the Roper Organization to determine what role American parents play in their children's reading development.

Publications

RIF Newsletter, a quarterly; *The RIF Guide to Encouraging Young Readers,* descriptions of 200 activities for parents and children with recommendations of popular books and resources for its audience; *When We Were Young,* the results of a survey of favorite children's books of public figures, celebrities, and RIF volunteers underwritten by Readers Digest Foundation to commemorate 1987 as the Year of the Reader; and booklets and instructional pamphlets.

Sources of Support

Private contributions with administrative support from the Smithsonian Institution.

§86 Reading Rainbow

601 West Fiftieth Street—Penthouse
New York, New York 10019
212-977-9100
Laura M. Frame, *Publicity/Outreach Coordinator*
Introduced in 1983

What/For Whom

Reading Rainbow is a PBS summer television series that is designed to motivate children to read. The productions mark one of the first collaborations of the publishing and television worlds to promote reading by young viewers coast to coast. Hosted by LeVar Burton, who achieved national television prominence in "Roots," the series has a half-hour magazine format that features an adaptation of a children's book; a field segment that explores places or ideas mentioned in the book; and reviews by children in the studio audience of three books of related interest. Celebrity narrators featured on the show include Peter Falk, Phylicia Rashad, Bill Cosby, and Gilda Radner. Animation, music, and on-location documentary sequences expand each book's theme to encourage young readers to see books as a part of their everyday lives.

The Association for Library Service to Children, a division of the American Library Association (§12), served on the project's advisory council with the National PTA (§77), the Association for Supervision and Curriculum Development, and the International Reading Association (§57). The series is a production of

Great Plains National/Nebraska Educational TV Network/University of Nebraska-Lincoln and WNED-TV, Buffalo, and is produced by Lancit Media Productions, Limited, in New York.

Examples

1) In 1989 Reading Rainbow, in cooperation with the Center for the Book in the Library of Congress (§32), is sponsoring brief television announcements promoting the Year of the Young Reader. The announcements, which feature LeVar Burton, are supported by Kellogg's.

2) A 1987 episode featured the book *Meanwhile Back at the Ranch* by Trinka Hakes Noble and illustrated by Tony Ross. LeVar experienced the Old West as he rode a stagecoach across the Arizona desert and visited Old Tucson, an authentic western town. He also received a taste of life as a cowboy when he donned true western garb, complete with spurs, chaps, and an official ten-gallon hat.

3) In 1986, Reading Rainbow featured science programming for the first time with grants underwritten by the Carnegie Corporation of New York and the National Science Foundation.

Publications

Reading Rainbow Gazette, a sixteen-page activity magazine that includes games, puzzles, and photographs from the series as well as a complete Reading Rainbow booklist; other specially written materials designed to help parents, libraries, and public television stations to encourage children to read when not in school.

Sources of Support

Funding from the Corporation for Public Broadcasting, the nation's public television stations, and the National Science Foundation.

§87 Reading Reform Foundation

949 Market Street, Suite 436
Tacoma, Washington 98402
206-572-9966
Marian S. Hinds, *President*
Established in 1961

What/For Whom

The Reading Reform Foundation is a national nonprofit educational organization committed to restoring literacy "by returning the alphabet, phonics first, to the teaching of reading." The membership believes that almost every child, regardless of social and economic background, can learn to read, write, and spell if taught by effective methods. The foundation also focuses on intensive phonics for older students and adults, disseminates information on the reading crisis and phonetics through local support groups; sponsors workshops and an clearinghouse and technical assistance to remedial reading programs; and gives testimony before groups.

Examples

1) The New York Metropolitan Area Chapter offers workshops for parents aimed primarily at getting children ready to learn to read. These courses also include some tips for helping older children with schoolwork.

2) In 1988, the seventh annual Conference of the New York City Metropolitan Chapter focused on "Effective Techniques for Teaching Reading, Writing, and Spelling."

Publications

The Reading Informer, a quarterly newsletter and various manuals, videotape cassettes; booklets; and articles.

Sources of Support

Membership dues, sale of publications and donations, grants from foundations, and individual contributions.

---

§88   Society for Scholarly Publishing (SSP)

1918 Eighteenth Street, N.W., Suite 21
Washington, D.C. 20009
202-328-3555
Alice O'Leary, *Administrative Officer*
Founded in 1979

What/For Whom

The Society for Scholarly Publishing is a national organization serving the scholarly publishing community as a whole. Its membership includes university presses, for-profit scholarly and professional presses, professional associations, museums, reference and database publishers, printers, individuals who work in these areas, librarians, and other information professionals. SSP provides for communication among these professionals, gives educational seminars, and in general helps its members to keep abreast of publishing trends, both technological and managerial/administrative. SSP holds an annual meeting in addition to its seminars.

Examples

1) "Marketing and Distribution of Scholarly Publications" is a day-and-a-half SSP seminar covering such topics as planning, marketing online services, and marketing books and journals.

2) The theme for the tenth annual meeting (1988) was "Scholarly Publishing: An Endangered Species."

Publications	SSP's *Letter,* published six times a year, carries SSP news, announcements of publications and book reviews, an international calendar of relevant conferences, meetings, and seminars, and other articles, *Scholarly Publishing,* a quarterly, and the proceedings of its annual meeting are also published regularly.
Sources of Support	Membership fees, grants from foundations and revenues from meetings and seminars.

---

§89   Society of Children's Book Writers (SCBW)

P.O. Box 296, Mar Vista Station
Los Angeles, California 90066
818-347-2849
Lin Oliver, *Executive Director*
Established in 1968

What/For Whom	The Society of Children's Book Writers is a professional organization for writers and illustrators of children's literature designed to offer a variety of services to people who write, illustrate, or share a vital interest in children's literature. SCBW acts as a network for the exchange of knowledge between children's writers, illustrators, editors, publishers, agents, librarians, educators, bookstore personnel, and others involved with literature for young people.
Examples	1) SCBW annually sponsors a national conference devoted entirely to writing and illustrating literature for children.
	2) The society administers a free manuscript exchange so that SCBW members can obtain professional criticism and feedback on their works in progress.
	3) SCBW awards Golden Kite statuettes each year for excellence in the field of children's books and presents magazine merit awards for outstanding original magazine work for young people during that year written or illustrated by SCBW members.
Publications	*SCBW Bulletin,* a bimonthly containing comprehensive and current information in the field of children's literature, and occasional monographs.
Source of Support	Membership dues.

§90 Southern Baptist Convention-Home Mission Board

Literacy Missions Ministries
1350 Spring Street, N.W.
Atlanta, Georgia 30367-5601
404-873-4041
Mildred Blankenship, *Assistant Director, Church and Community Ministries*
Established in 1959

What/For Whom

The Home Mission Board of the Southern Baptist Convention promotes and develops literacy training programs through Southern Baptist churches and associations around the country. Literacy is seen as a mission rather than a social service. The ministries train volunteer tutors to work in adult literacy programs, in programs for school-age children and youth, and in English as a second language.

Publications

Handbook for Literacy Missions, which outlines the ministries' rationale and procedures for teaching reading, writing, and conversational English, and other training resources.

Source of Support

The Southern Baptist Church.

§91 Special Libraries Association (SLA)

1700 Eighteenth Street, N.W.
Washington, D.C. 20009
202-234-4700
David Malinak, *Director of Communications*
Founded in 1909

What/For Whom

Special Libraries Association is a nonprofit, international professional organization of more than 12,500 members who work in special libraries serving corporate, research, government, technical, and academic institutions that use or produce specialized information. The primary goal of the association is to advance the leadership role of the special librarian/information professional by providing a variety of services to enhance members' professional skills and advance the interests of the special libraries community. SLA is made up of fifty-five regional chapters, twenty-eight subject divisions, and numerous committees. The association holds an annual conference and other meetings; conducts continuing education programs; administers scholarships, grants, and awards; and provides other services of benefit to its membership.

Examples

1) The chapters, as the local units of SLA, have meetings often featuring guest speakers, professional events, or special social activities. In 1987, the Eastern Canada chapter used their holiday social to raise money for the Kenya library book fund, and the Southern California chapter sponsored a "Save the Books" dinner for the fire-ravaged Los Angeles Public Library.

2) The divisions serve members' technical and subject interests through educational programs, publications, and cooperative projects with other information-related organizations. SLA divisions include advertising and marketing, business and finance, education, engineering, environmental information, library management, metals/materials, military librarians, museums, the arts, newspapers, nuclear science, publishing, and telecommunications.

3) The theme of the seventy-ninth annual conference (1988) was "Expanding Horizons: Strategies for Information Managers."

Publications

SpeciaList, a monthly newsletter, informs members and other readers of association news, events taking place in the information community, and current developments in the field, *Special Libraries* is a quarterly scholarly journal and *Who's Who in Special Libraries,* the annual membership directory, Monographs and pamphlets are also published. Each chapter publishes its own newsletter and the divisions also produce books and other publications that address a variety of specialized topics.

Sources of Support

Membership dues, contributions from foundations and corporations, and sale of publications.

---

§92 Television Information Office (TIO)

National Association of Broadcasters
745 Fifth Avenue
New York, New York 10151
212-759-6800
Roy E. Mulholland, Director
Established in 1959; to close permanently on March 31, 1989.

What/For Whom

The Television Information Office is a research, education, and information center maintained by the television industry for the public, the press, and broadcasters. TIO presents the strengths and values of free over-the-air television to society, addresses the issues raised by critics of the television industry, protects the economic values of free over-the-air television, and commissions research on public attitudes toward television. In September 1988, TIO board members voted to shut it down in 1989, citing financial constraints and declining membership.

Publications

Among research projects TIO has commissioned and the many publications currently available are a series of ongoing national surveys, directed by the Roper Organization, about changing public attitudes toward television. *America's Watching Public Attitudes toward Television,* released in 1987, is the fifteenth in this series of studies. Other material distributed by TIO focuses on television and children and television's impact on society.

Sources of Support

TIO is supported by the three major television networks (ABC, CBS, NBC), individual television stations and groups, the National Association of Broadcasters, and the Station Representatives Association. Additional funding comes from the sale of publications.

---

§93   Unesco Section for Book Promotion Division for the Arts, Cultural Exchanges, and Book Promotion

Unesco
7, Place de Fontenoy
75700 Paris, France
33-45.68.10.00
Marcia Lord, *Chief of Section*

What/For Whom

The efforts of Unesco's Section for Book Promotion continue to be aimed at goals set at the 1982 World Congress on Books. The congress, whose theme was "Towards a Reading Society," emphasized national development of publishing and book distribution systems, the creation of a reading environment for all ages at all levels of society, and international publishing cooperation and book trade. Consequently, the section's priorities include programs to train editors, booksellers, book designers, printers, and other book workers in areas where the book trade is underdeveloped; financial and technical support for nations studying and improving national book policies and book distribution systems; the organization of national reading campaigns; assistance in providing reading materials for new literates; research into national problems in the book world and into the future of the book; and reading promotion for particular groups such as children, the disadvantaged, rural populations, families, the handicapped, and the blind.

Unesco also supports regional centers for both promotion and development for Latin America and the Caribbean (CERLALC), headquartered in Bogota, Columbia; Africa South

114

of the Sahara (CREPLA), in Yaounde, Cameroun; and Asia and the Pacific (ACCU), in Tokyo. The organization is currently assisting a number of developing countries, including Ivory Coast, Madagascar, and Malaysia, in organizing for a "Year of the Reader" and is laying the groundwork for International Literacy Year in 1990.

Examples

1) A Centre for the Production of Reading Materials for the Blind has been established at Kenyatta University in Nairobi, Kenya, with assistance from Unesco and its International Programme for the Development of Communication (IPDC). Equipment, materials, training, and technical assistance have been provided.

2) University-level training courses in publishing and related book fields have been created with Unesco's assistance in Colombia, Ghana, and the Philippines, with a number of others in various stages of development.

Publications

The section publishes a series of studies on national and international book development. One of these, published in 1984, *The Future of the Book, Part III: New Technologies in Book Distribution: The United States Experience,* was prepared by the Center for the Book in the Library of Congress (§32). Recent titles include *Books and Reading in Tanzania* and *Books and Reading in India.*

Source of Support

Unesco.

§94 U.S. Department of Commerce

Washington, D.C. 20230
202-377-0379
William S. Lofquist, *Industry Specialist,*
International Trade Administration—Printing and Publishing

What/For Whom

Four agencies within the Department of Commerce engage in activities of particular interest to the book community.

1) Through its Bureau of Census and other agencies, the Department of Commerce keeps statistics on United States publishing and the reading public. The department notes, "The nation's concern with improving reading and educational skills should help the U.S. book industry...As the country's economy shifts toward services and away from goods production, the educational requirements of the workforce take on increased importance." Statistics on newspapers, periodicals, and books trace present and projected developments in the areas of printing, publishing, graphic arts, labor and material costs, advertising, and sales.

2) The **International Trade Administration (ITA)** was established in January 1980 to promote world trade and to strength the international trade and investment position of the United States. Its functions include (a) export promotion-trade exhibits, trade missions, catalog and video displays, and the rental of overseas trade centers, (b) formation of trade policy—including the protection of U.S. intellectual property overseas, and (c) trade analysis—studies of trade barriers, publication of trade data, and preparation of the annual *U.S. Industrial Outlook,* which consists of economic reviews and forecasts on the U.S. book publishing industry.

3) The **National Institute of Standards and Technology** (formerly National Bureau of Standards) supplies the measurement foundation for U.S. industry science and technology. Since 1979, the bureau has trained librarians from developing countries in technical and scientific librarianship. For additional information, contact the Information Resources and Services Division, 301-975-3058.

4) The **National Technical Information Service (NTIS)** is the central source for the public sale and distribution of government-sponsored research, development and engineering reports, foreign technical reports, and reports prepared by local government agencies. Periodicals database files, computer programs, and U.S. government-owned patent applications are also available. Anyone may search the NTIS Bibliographic Data online, using the services of organizations that maintain the database for public use through contractual relationships with NTIS. The agency is self-supporting in that all costs of its products and services are paid from sales income. For additional information, contact the NTIS Office of Customer Services, 703-487-4660.

Publications

Census of Manufactures, Annual Survey of Manufactures, and *County Business Patterns,* published on a periodic basis by the Bureau of the Census, contain extensive statistics on U.S. book publishing (statistically classified as industry 2731). The *U.S. Industrial Outlook,* published annually by the International Trade Administration, contains economic analyses and projections on the book publishing industry. Full summaries of current U.S. and foreign research reports are published regularly by NTIS in a wide variety of weekly newsletters, a biweekly journal, an annual index, and various subscription formats.

Source of Support

Federal government.

§95

U. S. Department of Education

400 Maryland Avenue, S.W.
Washington, D.C. 20202
202-245-3192

What/For Whom

The Department of Education establishes policies for administrators and coordinates most federal assistance to education. The secretary of education advises the President on education plans, policies, and programs of the federal government. The secretary directs department staff in carrying out the approved activities and promotes public understanding of the department's objectives and programs. Several offices and divisions within the Department of Education conduct programs of special interest to the book community.

Examples

1) **Adult Literacy Initiative** was established in 1983 to work both within the government and outside of it to combat illiteracy among youths and adults who are out of school. The initiative is intended to serve and coordinate federal literacy activities in the Department of Education and other departments and agencies, to encourage state and local literacy initiatives, and to promote corporate and union participation in literacy efforts. It also cooperates with the Coalition for Literacy (§39).

The College Work-Study program is an effort to coordinate intra-agency activities by redirecting existing department resources to adult literacy. What began as a pilot activity has continued with the idea of giving additional (supplemental) money to schools with established Adult Literacy Programs. Fifty-six institutions received supplemental awards in 1987-88.

Federal Employee Literacy Training Program (FELT) was created through the Federal Interagency Committee on Education. FELT recruits volunteers for local literacy programs from federal agencies in all regions of the country and locates available federal space for use by literacy programs. The initiative has also produced a short videotape on FELT for use by participating agencies in their recruitment efforts.

The Update (formerly *ALI Update*) published quarterly, features Department of Education programs, major federally funded adult literacy research programs and projects, and other national literacy news. The newsletter results from the combined efforts of Adult Literacy Initiative and the Division of Adult Education.

For additional information, contact Karl O. Haigler, Director of Adult Literacy Initiative, 202-732-2959.

2) **Center for Statistics** gathers, analyzes, and synthesizes data on the characteristics and performance of American education. The areas covered include public and nonpublic elementary and secondary education; postsecondary education, including college and university libraries; and vocational and adult education.

3) **Clearinghouse on Adult Education,** established in 1981, provides information and referral services in the area of adult education, including literacy and English as a second language. The U.S. Department of Education Adult Literacy Initiative has served as a catalyst for the clearinghouse's ongoing work.

Clearinghouse publications include *Bibliography of Resource Materials* which has sections on literacy, English as a second language, and "Older Persons"; handbooks; catalog of nationally validated adult education programs; literacy materials; and informational brochures.

For additional information, contact Patricia Lang, 202-732-2396.

4) **Education Resources Information Center (ERIC),** founded in 1966, is a national system that collects and disseminates findings of research and development and descriptions of exemplary programs in various education fields. ERIC clearinghouses are operated under federal contracts by education organizations and institutions around the country. ERIC is a major database center for fugitive information on reading, English, speech, journalism, theater, and related communication fields. The clearinghouses or centers collect, evaluate, abstract, and index hard-to-find educational literature; conduct computer searches; commission studies; and act as resource guides. The information collected is listed in the network's reference publications and indexed in extensive computerized files. Each of the sixteen clearinghouses or centers is responsible for a particular educational area. More than seven hundred educational institutions, roughly one-tenth of them abroad, carry the entire ERIC collection and make it available to the public. The clearinghouses are operated under federal contract with the Department of Education. For two examples, see §30 and §44.

ERIC prepares the reference periodical *Resources in Education* (RIE), a monthly journal containing abstracts of each educational item that ERIC collects and makes to current educational periodicals containing ERIC annotations of journal articles.

5) **Library Programs,** formed in 1985, administers nine grant programs, which are authorized by two laws: the Library Services and Construction Act (LSCA) and the Higher Education Act (HEA). Library Programs' support is used to provide seed money for innovative or experimental programs, assist literacy projects, encourage the development of services to disadvantaged populations, provide financial incentives to libraries to share resources, and conduct evaluations and research on library issues.

In 1987, in cooperation with the Center for the Book in the Library of Congress (§32), Library Programs cosponsored a project for high school students titled "Leaders are Readers."

Library Programs worked with American Library Association (§12) and National Commission on Libraries and Information Science (§70) on a "Campaign for Libraries" to ensure that every child has a library card by the end of the 1988-89 school year.

In 1988, Library Programs published *Library Literacy Program: Analysis of Funded Projects*.

For additional information, contact Anne J. Mathews, Director of Library Programs, 202-357-6293.

6) **Office of Bilingual Education and Minority Languages Affairs** works for equal educational opportunity and improved programs for "limited proficiency and minority languages populations" by providing support for programs, activities, and management initiatives that meet their special needs for bilingual education. The office administers the Bilingual Education: Family English Literacy Program which provides grants to local educational agencies, institutions of higher education, and private nonprofit organizations to establish, operate, and improve family English literacy programs.

7) **Office of Educational Research and Improvement (OERI)** supports and conducts research on education, collects and analyzes education statistics, administers grant and contract programs to improve libraries and library education, and disseminates information to parents, students, teachers, and others. See Office of Research, Center for Statistics, and Library Programs for descriptions of three program offices which carry out the work of OERI.

8) **Office of Research (OR)** supports the scholarly and academic work of individuals and institutions. The research is designed to advance knowledge about educational practice and is aimed at solving or alleviating specific educational problems. OR supports the educational research and development centers which have been established to conduct research in several areas including teaching, learning, teacher education, writing, and reading. The Reading Research and Education Center is one example (see §33).

9) **Vocational and Adult Education** provides grants, contracts, and technical assistance for vocational and technical education, professions development in education, community schools, and comprehensive employment and training. It also funds on a matching basis the Adult Basic Education Program (ABE), one of the largest adult basic skills programs in the nation launched in 1964. It is administered at the state level by state education agencies and at the local level by school districts and uses paid instructors and some volunteer tutors. The ABE program provides instruction in reading, writing, and other basic skills, including English as a second language.

The Division of Adult Education, part of Vocational and Adult Education, is a coproducer with Adult Literacy Initiative of *The Update*, a newsletter for the adult literacy and learning community. In 1988, the division issued the publication: *The Bottom Line: Basic Skills in the Workplace*.

Source of Support Federal government.

---

§96 U.S. Information Agency (USIA)

301 4th Street, S.W.
Washington, D.C. 20547
202-485-2866
Philip W. Pillsbury, *Acting Director, Cultural Centers and Resources*

What/For Whom The United States Information Agency is responsible for the government's overseas information and cultural programs. Several of its activities are of special concern to the book community, including the USIA library, book export, translation, exhibits, and book donation programs. Several of these programs are reviewed in the Center for the Book in the Library of Congress (§32) publication, *U.S. Books Abroad: Neglected Ambassadors* (1984), by Curtis G. Benjamin. The USIA also encourages person-to-person exchanges that sometimes include publishers, librarians, and booksellers.

Examples 1) USIA maintains 138 libraries and reading rooms in 84 countries and also provides support for library programs in binational centers in 17 countries. The focus of these collections is on materials that will help people in foreign countries learn about the United States, its people, history, culture, and political and social processes. For further information, contact Richard Fitz, chief, Library Program Division, 202-485-2915.

2) The Book Program Division organizes exhibits of American books for major international book fairs. This division also assembles exhibits of appropriate American publications for overseas professional events, seminars, libraries, and scholarly institutions. For further information, contact Robert McLaughlin, Chief, Book Program Division, 202-485-2896.

3) The U.S. Information Agency Private Sector Book and Library Advisory Committee advises the USIA on its book and library programs.

4) The Library/Book Fellows program was initiated in 1986 with a USIA grant to the American Library Association (§12). The purpose of the program is to place American library and

publishing professionals in foreign institutions or organizations for periods of several months to a year to carry out projects identified as important to U.S. and host-country interests. Projects include organizing a law collection, school library development, and compiling a list of U.S. books translated into Arabic.

5) In cooperation with the Center for the Book in the Library of Congress, the USIA is sponsoring a U.S.-Soviet "1989—Year of the Young Reader" special initiative during 1989.
Major elements include an exchange of children's books exhibits and publication of translations of children's books of both countries.

Source of Support   Federal government.

---

§97   Urban Literacy Network

7505 Metro Boulevard
Minneapolis, Minnesota 55435
612-893-7661
Jean E. Hammink, *Project Director*
Established in 1986

What/For Whom

The Urban Literacy Network is a broadly representative national leadership organization which supports the development and enhancement of strong urban literacy agendas. It does so by working to engage public and private constituencies in the formulation and implementation of literacy policies, plans and programs for urban areas; encouraging and assisting the development of coordinated urban initiatives; focusing national, state, and local public and private sector resources to provide sufficient and ongoing support for urban literacy efforts; and advocating federal, state, and local delivery systems that provide a wide range of literacy services. The network provides technical assistance and training to demonstration projects funded through its grants program and to cooperative literacy efforts that are developing or are under way in other areas. Technical assistance services include retreat planning and facilitation, on-site consultation, exchange visits, and topical training. The network convenes meetings and makes presentations at other national and state conferences to raise and discuss urban literacy issues and directions.

Examples

1) The network developed a broad-based computerized national literacy clearinghouse and resource file in partnership with United Way of America and the Literacy Assistance Center in New York.

2) The January 1988 National Conference on Urban Literacy was held to provide information, training, and networking opportunities for all those working to ensure adequate and effective literacy services to adults in urban areas.

Publications

The network provides monthly written information to its funded projects; publishes *Issues,* a newsletter; and is compiling a resource directory derived from a survey of urban cooperative efforts.

Sources of Support

Funds from the federal government, foundations, and corporations.

---

§98

White House Conference on Library and Information Services Task Force (WHCLIST)

236 Freeman Parkway
Providence, Rhode Island 02906
401-272-7745
Joan Reeves, *Chair*
Founded in 1979

What/For Whom

WHCLIST promotes and monitors the implementation of the resolutions of the 1979 White House Conference on Libraries and Information Services. WHCLIST membership includes two delegates from each state, one a professional and the other a lay delegate. In addition, six voting delegates are selected from each state to participate during the annual meeting. WHCLIST has over 565 dues paying members. In general, the 1979 White House conference promoted the value of library and information service as a national resource. It debated and adopted sixty-four resolutions ranging in subject from support for freedom of speech, to access to information, to school libraries, and to international information exchange. In support of these resolutions, WHCLIST monitors progress at the national and state levels, testifies at state and congressional hearings on relevant issues, and promotes citizen involvement in friends of libraries groups and other cultural organizations.

Examples

1) WHCLIST annually compiles a *Report from the States* that details progress toward implementation of the White House conference resolutions. A national five-year review was also prepared in 1984 and updated in 1985.

2) WHCLIST sponsors awards for the Outstanding Legislator, the Outstanding Citizen, and the Outstanding Publication of the year.

3) At its annual meeting in August 1988, WHCLIST formed several focus groups to develop recommendations for the National Commission on Libraries and Information Science (§70) and the White House Conference Advisory Committee addressing themes and issues for the second White House Conference, which is to be held between September 1, 1989, and September 1991.

Publications

Annual *Report from the States, WHCLIST L.I.S.T.E.N.* (Library and Information Services Educational Newsletter), and the five-year review.

Sources of Support

Associate members' fees and contributions and grants.

---

§99 Women of the Evangelical Lutheran Church in America

8765 West Higgins Road
Chicago, Illinois 60631
312-380-2736
Faith L. Fretheim, *Director for Literacy*

What/For Whom

The Women of the Evangelical Lutheran Church in America (ECLA), formerly Lutheran Church Women, support literacy under their Mission: Action programming. Under it, the Volunteer Reading Aides (VRA) Program was established in 1968 and is the nation's largest ecumenical literacy and or English-as-a-Second-Language project. VRA trains volunteer tutors, organizes community-based literacy programs where none already exist, conducts literacy workshops for libraries and community agencies, and provides literacy referral and general information services to the church and the general public. Non-members of the Evangelical Lutheran Church of America are welcomed both as tutors and students. Other literacy activities include an advocacy network and a public awareness campaign. Lutheran bookstores in eighteen cities have agreed to distribute several literacy titles produced by ELCA at low cost.

Examples

1) Through VRA, training is offered to professional teachers in the principles of teaching English to speakers of other languages (ESOL).

2) The VRA program has helped migrant and native Canadian groups select and write materials suited to specialized literacy needs.

Publications   The VRA program develops and publishes inexpensive, easy-to-read materials for new readers and ESOL students, and resource materials for tutors and literacy program leaders.

Sources of Support   Donations from Women of the Evangelical Lutheran Church and other church members; sale of publications, films, and videotapes, and service fees from groups requesting assistance.

---

§100   Women's National Book Association (WNBA)

160 Fifth Avenue, Room 604
New York, New York 10010
212-675-7805
Marie Cantlon, *President*
Founded in 1917

What/For Whom   The Women's National Book Association is open to men and women in all occupations allied to the publishing industry. WNBA aims at strengthening the status of women in the book industry, sponsoring studies and educational sessions toward this end. WNBA sponsors awards for women in the book industry and for sellers of children's books. WNBA has active chapters in Binghamton, Boston, Detroit, Los Angeles, Nashville, New York, San Francisco, and Washington.

Examples   1) The Women's National Book Association Award (formerly the Constance Lindsay Skinner Award) honors women in the book world who have made a difference in bringing authors and their readers together. For its seventieth anniversary (1987), WNBA saluted seventy notable women in the book world "who have made a difference" as the WNBA Book Women Award winners. The Washington chapter cosponsored a program and reception with the Center for the Book in the Library of Congress (§32) to honor the Washington area WNBA Book Women Award winners and to celebrate 1987 as the Year of the Reader.

2) The Lucile Micheels Pannell Award is given annually to a bookseller whose efforts bring children and books together.

Publications   *The Bookwoman* is published three times a year; individual chapters publish newsletters as well.

Sources of Support   Membership fees. Publishing companies may become "sustaining members."

A Few Other Resources

A number of resources are too important to pass by completely but did not fit neatly into our main list of organizations. Here we note a number of publications and organizations that also belong to the community of the book, a community, as the arrangement of this section illustrates, that stretches from author and publisher to reader and promoter. Two essential publications should be noted at the outset: *Literary Market Place: The Directory of American Book Publishing* (LMP), published by R.R. Bowker toward the end of each calendar year (LMP 1989 appeared in December 1988) and *The Bowker Annual of Library and Book Trade Information* (the *Bowker Annual*), published by Bowker each spring (the thirty-third edition appeared in May 1988).

Authors and writing. Societies for the study and appreciation of individual authors abound. The 1989 edition of the *Encyclopedia of Associations,* for example, lists over 120. Mark Twain alone has inspired the formation of 6 U.S. organizations. *Literary Market Place* lists 99 organizations under the heading "Literary and Writers' Associations." It also lists 161 writers conferences and workshops. Detailed information about writers' "colonies and retreats" can be found in *The Guide to Writers Conferences, Seminars, Colonies, Retreats, and Organizations* (Shaw Associates, 1988). Several states and many large cities have organizations that support the interests of local writers; examples include the Arizona Authors Association, the Nebraska Writers Guild, the Independent Writers of Chicago, and Washington Independent Writers. *Writer's Northwest Handbook: A Guide to the Northwest's Writing and Publishing Industry* (Media Weavers, 3d ed., 1988) is an important regional directory. The monthly *Writer's Digest* (F&W Publications, Inc.) addresses concerns of prospective writers. The quarterly *Visible Language,* published by the Rhode Island School of Design, "is concerned with research and ideas that help define the unique role and properties of written language." Also see main entries for Authors League of America, Inc., and Authors Guild, Inc. (§22), Literary Landmarks Association (§62), PEN American Center (§80), Poets & Writers, Inc. (§82), and Society of Children's Book Writers (§89).

Publishing. *Publishers Weekly* (Cahners/R.R. Bowker, New York) is the trade magazine of the U.S. book industry. Its subtitle is "the international news magazine of book publishing." Its articles deal with all aspects of the book trade and its advertisements announce publications, advertising plans, printing services, and management services. *Small Press: The Magazine and Review of Independent Publishing* (Meckler Publishing Co.), published five times a year, is devoted to news of the small press world and reviews of small press books. The Small Press Center in New York City publishes a useful newsletter. Other periodicals, such as *Scholarly Publishing* (University of Toronto Press), *Microform Review* (Meckler Publishing), *Fine Print* (San Francisco), and *Desktop Publishing* (Redwood City, Calif.) treat specialized aspects of publishing. Statistics about the book trade can be found in the Book Industry Study Group's *Book Industry Trends* as well as in the section on "Book Trade

Research and Statistics" in *The Bowker Annual of Library and Book Trade Information*. Courses for students interested in learning about the book trade are taught at several universities, including New York University, Stanford University, and Radcliffe College. A listing under the heading "Courses for the Book Trade" is found in *Literary Market Place* (Bowker), the annual directory of the book trade that includes publishers, book clubs, literary agents, book distributors, book trade, writers' and press associations, wholesalers, book manufacturers, paper suppliers, binders, and much more. Bowker also publishes *International Literary Market Place*, which provides similar information on a world scale. Also see main entries for the American Newspaper Publishers Association Foundation (§13), Association of American Publishers, Inc. (§19), Association of American University Presses, Inc. (§20), Book Industry Study Group, Inc. (§24), International Publishers Association (§56), and Society for Scholarly Publishing (§88).

Book production and design. There are many groups, in addition to those organizations listed in the main section of this directory, that exchange ideas and sponsor programs and projects about the manufacturing, design, and production of books. The list includes Bookbinders of New York; Bookbuilders of Boston; Bookbuilders of Washington; the Pyramid Atlantic Center for Papers, Prints, and Books (Baltimore and Washington); and the Chicago-based Society of Typographic Arts, which publishes an annual, the *STA Design Journal*. For an extensive listing, see the "Book Trade and Allied Associations" section of *Literary Market Place*. See also main entries for the American Institute of Graphic Arts (§10), Book Manufacturers' Institute (§25), Bookbuilders West (§26), Center for Book Arts (§31), Chicago Book Clinic (§34), Minnesota Center for Book Arts (§63), and Philadelphia Book Clinic (§81).

Book arts. Interest in the study and preservation of book arts such as typography, printing, binding, design and graphics, and papermaking has increased during the past decade. Book arts programs are now offered at more than two dozen colleges and universities around the country. Graduate degrees can be pursued at the University of Alabama, Mills College, and the University of the Arts in Philadelphia. *Fine Print: The Review of the Arts of the Book* (San Francisco) chronicles the resurgence of the book arts and small press movement of which it is such a vital part. Also see main entries for the American Institute of Graphic Arts (§10), Center for Book Arts (§31), and Minnesota Center for Book Arts (§63).

Book preservation. Book condition studies conducted in the nation's largest and oldest research libraries have shown that a significant percentage of our printed intellectual heritage (some 25 percent) is deteriorating from the problem of acid degradation of the paper. Most affected are books printed from 1840 to 1920. A number of organizations have joined forces to call attention to the problem of "brittle books," and to conduct cooperative preservation projects to save the most important materials from extinction. Most significant is increasing advocacy for the use of long-lasting, alkaline paper. *An American National Standard for Permanent Paper for Printed Library Materials* was published by the National Information Standards Organization in 1984 and most university presses now publish on alkaline paper. In 1988 the New York Public Library established the Center for Paper Permanency. An independent group, Authors and Publishers in Support of Preservation of the Printed Word, solicits commitments from authors to have their first editions printed on permanent paper. In 1988 Senator Claiborne Pell introduced a joint resolution calling for a "National Policy on Permanent Paper." These national movements are being echoed by the states, several of which have established state offices for preservation. Publications that describe preservation activities include *The Abbey Newsletter* (Abbey Publications), *Conservation Administration News* (University of Tulsa Libraries), and *National Preservation News* (Library of Congress). Also see main entries for the Council on Library Resources (§43), Library of Congress (§60), and the National Information Standards Organization (§76).

Book history. The study of the history of books and the effect of books, reading, and printing on society is a rapidly growing field. Important descriptions of the range of topics and resources being explored include *Needs and Opportunities in the History of the Book: America, 1639-1876* (American Antiquarian Society, 1987), and Alice D. Schreyer's *The History of Books: A Guide to Selected Resources in the Library of Congress* (Library of Congress, 1987). The Library History Roundtable of the American Library Association (ALA) and the History of Reading SIG of the International Reading Association (IRA) are two of the professional groups contributing to this new area of scholarly endeavor. Also see main entries for American Antiquarian Society (§4), American Printing History Association (§14), Bibliographical Society of America (§23), and Center for the Book in the Library of Congress (§32).

Rare books. The Rare Books and Manuscripts Section of the Association of College and Research Libraries (ACRL) of the American Library Association is the major professional force in this field. The ACRL journal, *Rare Books and Manuscripts,* published twice a year, deals with current trends, issues, and publications. Each summer the Rare Book School of the Columbia University School of Library Service, organized by Terry Belanger, brings experts and students together. *Rare Books 1983-84: Trends, Collections, Sources,* edited by Alice D. Schreyer and published by R.R. Bowker in 1984, is a valuable guide and resource which includes lists of appraisers of books and manuscripts, auctioneers of literary property, and dealers in antiquarian books and manuscripts. Also of value is the pamphlet *Your Old Books* by Peter Van Wingen, published by the ACRL. Also see main entries for the American Antiquarian Society (§4), Antiquarian Booksellers Association of America (§16), Center for the Book in the Library of Congress (§32), and the Library of Congress (§60).

Book collecting. Book collecting clubs around the country sponsor a wide variety of programs, exhibitions, lectures, and publications on book collecting, rare books, fine printing, the graphic arts, and related topics. Major clubs include the Grolier Club in New York, founded in 1884; the Club of Odd Volumes in Boston; The Rowfant Club in Cleveland; the Caxton Club in Chicago; the Zamorano Club in Los Angeles; the Book Club of California and the Roxburghe Club in San Francisco; the Baltimore Bibliophiles; and the Pittsburgh Bibliophiles. Two volumes edited by Jean Peters, *Book Collecting: A Modern Guide* (Bowker, 1977) and *Collectible Books: Some New Paths* (Bowker, 1979), provide a comprehensive introduction to book collecting.

Bookselling. *Publishers Weekly* contains much of interest, and *American Bookseller* (American Booksellers Association) is the basic trade magazine. The *American Book Trade Directory* (Bowker) lists bookstores and book wholesalers. Regional book trade organizations and associations exist in most areas. Many parts of *Literary Market Place* are relevant to the bookselling business as well as to publishing. The antiquarian/rare book trade relies on *AB/Bookman's Weekly* (Clifton, N. J.), a valuable resource that also carries news about current happenings throughout the book world. Also see main entries for the American Booksellers Association (§7), Antiquarian Booksellers Association of America (§16), Association of Booksellers for Children (§21), Christian Booksellers Association (§38), and National Association of College Stores (§66).

Libraries. *Library Journal* (Bowker), *American Libraries* (American Library Association), *Wilson Library Bulletin* (H.W. Wilson Company), and *Special Libraries* (Special Libraries Association) are principal sources of news and information. In addition, associations, university departments, and professional publishers produce a great number of journals and newsletters for particular areas of librarianship. The *ALA Yearbook of Library and Information Services* (American Library Association) provides an annual review of events and of the activities of many library professional groups. The *Bowker Annual of Library and Book Trade Information* (Bowker) includes sections on library legislation, funding, and grants, as well as a directory of library organizations and a calendar of important upcoming events. Also see main entries for the American Library Association (§12), Council on Library Resources, Inc.(§43), Friends of Libraries U.S.A. (§47), International Federation of Library Associations and Institutions (§55), Library of Congress (§60), and Special Libraries Association (§91).

Book reviewing. Only a small percentage of the fifty-thousand or so books published each year in the United States are reviewed—or receive any kind of published notice. The "Book Review, Selection, and Reference" section of *Literary Market Place* lists book review journals and syndicates. Specialized journals review many books in their particular fields, but general book reviews such as the *New York Times Book Review* and the *Washington Post* and *Los Angeles Times* book sections become fewer each year.

Book awards. Awards are an increasingly popular means of recognizing achievement in the book world. Most of the awards honor authors, but others mark distinction in bookmaking and in the book professions. Information about awards can be found in *Literary Market Place, The Bowker Annual of Library and Book Trade Information,* and *Children's Literature Awards and Winners* (Neal-Schuman, 2d. ed., 1988). Also see main entries for the National Book Awards, Inc. (§67) and National Book Critics Circle (§68).

Book fairs, festivals, and exhibits. Major international book fairs such as the annual fairs in Frankfurt, Bologna, London, and Jerusalem are listed in *Literary Market Place's* section, "Calendar of Book Trade & Promotional Events." Book fairs are growing in popularity in the United States. Examples include New York is Book Country, the Miami Book Fair, the Milwaukee Book Fair, and the Minnesota Book Festival. The theme of the seventh annual Key West Literary Festival, held in January 1989, was "The Short Story." Children's book fairs are important, too. The Children's Literacy Initiative (Philadelphia), for example, organizes "Children's Expo," a fair that has been held in Indianapolis, Boston, and Oakland. School Book Fairs, Inc. (Worthington, Ohio) sponsors Kids Are Authors, an annual event to honor young authors. WaldenEd, a newly formed book fair company, is a subsidiary of Waldenbooks. Texas School Book Fairs is a division of Scholastic Book Fairs, Inc.

Literacy and reading promotion initiatives. Since the publication in 1983 of *A Nation at Risk,* the widely publicized report of the National Commission on Excellence in Education, there has been a dramatic increase in the number and kind of projects to combat illiteracy and motivate reading. The private sector, in particular, has become increasingly committed to aiding education, literacy, and reading promotion. This directory, in the main entries listed below, mentions many of the projects, both private and governmental. Additional examples include Pizza Hut's BOOK IT!, a national reading incentive program in elementary schools; Time, Inc.'s "Time to Read" literacy program; the Gannett Foundation's Literacy Challenge program; Jell-O Desserts' Reading Rocket project; Domino's Pizza's employee literacy program; and the "Erase Illiteracy-Read" campaign/billboard project initiated by the U.S. Government Printing Office. In addition, in 1986 a Congressional Task Force on Illiteracy, composed of members of the U.S. House of Representatives and the U.S. Senate, was formed to support legislative action on behalf of literacy. Also see main entries for the American Reading Council, Ltd. (§15), Assault on Illiteracy Program (§17), Association for Community-Based Education (§18), Business Council for Effective Literacy (§27), Cartoonists Across America (§29), Center for the Book in the Library of Congress (§32), Coalition for Literacy (§39), Contact Literacy Center (§40), Literacy Volunteers of America (§61), Project Literacy U.S. (§83), Push Literacy Action Now (§84), Reading Is Fundamental, Inc. (§85), Reading Reform Foundation (§87), U.S. Department of Education (§95), and Urban Literacy Network (§97).

Book culture promotion. Books, reading, and literacy promotion are active functions of government in most countries outside the United States. In Canada, for example, in September 1988 the government announced a major $110 million literacy initiative aimed at combating illiteracy through partnerships with provincial and territorial governments and community and voluntary organizations. In several countries, however, there are small, catalytic organizations that rely on a combination of private and government support to promote books and reading, organizations similar to the Center for the Book in the Library of Congress. Great Britain's Book Trust, for example, promotes "the role of books in the enhancement of life." Others are Australia's National Book Council, located in Carlton; the New Zealand Council, in Wellington; the Deutsche Lesegesellschaft, in Mainz, Federal Republic of Germany; and the Fundacion Germain Sanchez Ruiperez, in Salamanca, Spain. Two other organizations focus on the study of the history of books and their role in society: The Herzog August Bibliothek Wolfenbuttel, in Wolfenbuttel, Federal Republic of Germany, and the Institut d'Etude du Livre in Paris. Unesco also maintains a number of regional book promotion centers. The Unesco general conference has proclaimed 1990 to be International Literacy Year, a program linked to the formulation of a plan to help Unesco member states in all regions of the world "eradicate illiteracy by the year 2000."

Index

Information in "Is There a Community of the Book?" and "A Few Other Resources" is indexed to page numbers (p.), whereas information in the main body of organizations is indexed to section numbers (§). Section numbers in **boldface** indicate an entry devoted to that organization.

In addition to a few publications indexed here, almost every organization in the main list publishes a newsletter, which has been noted in the entry for that organization.